Helping Parents Understand the Minds and Hearts of Generation Z

OTHER BOOKS BY THE AUTHOR

The Entitled Generation: Helping Teachers Teach and Reach the Minds and Hearts of Generation Z (2017)

Common Sense Education: From Common Core to ESSA and Beyond (2016)

The Wrong Direction for Today's Schools: The Impact of Common Core on American Education (2015)

Teacher-Student Relationships: Crossing into the Emotional, Physical, and Sexual Realms (2013)

Helping Parents Understand the Minds and Hearts of Generation Z

Ernest J. Zarra III

ROWMAN & LITTLEFIELD
Lanham • Boulder • New York • London

Published by Rowman & Littlefield
A wholly owned subsidiary of The Rowman & Littlefield Publishing Group, Inc.
4501 Forbes Boulevard, Suite 200, Lanham, Maryland 20706
www.rowman.com

Unit A, Whitacre Mews, 26-34 Stannary Street, London SE11 4AB

British Library Cataloguing in Publication Information Available

Library of Congress Cataloging-in-Publication Data Available

ISBN 978-1-4758-3188-7 (hardcover)
ISBN 978-1-4758-3189-4 (paperback)
ISBN 978-1-4758-3190-0 (ebook)

∞™ The paper used in this publication meets the minimum requirements of
American National Standard for Information Sciences—Permanence of Paper
for Printed Library Materials, ANSI/NISO Z39.48-1992.

Printed in the United States of America

This book is dedicated to Jourdan Bacot,
"The Little Drummer Girl,"
whose Christmas story brought a community
to its knees . . .
December 25, 2016

Contents

Table

Preface

Writing a book for parents is quite humbling. All of us with children share similar experiences. Raising children is unique and among the most blessed experiences ever. Regardless of the number of children, no two are alike. That is the fun part: every day is an adventure.

Parenting is as humbling as it is exhilarating. Parenting can make you angry, and that anger can help a parent find the deepest of loves to be known. The moment a parent thinks he or she has it figured out, it is back to the drawing board. The moment the expected is supposed to occur, the unexpected rocks your world. Certainly, writing a book for parents can only be done with an understanding of what all parents have in common.

Whatever insights I have derived, come from personal experience and years of observation. I can honestly say that I became a better parent because I have been a teacher: I just wish it worked the other way around as well. One feature that most parents have in common—this author concluded—is that none of us are experts, although all of us pretend to be at one time or another. Another thing is for certain: children are experts at being children.

REASONS FOR WRITING THIS BOOK

The reasons for writing this book on helping parents to understand the hearts and minds of their Gen Z children are threefold. First, I am an educated parent, a husband of more than four decades, an educator for nearly four decades, an author, and a blogger. People expect me to know something about something. I can either fake it or make an effort to write something tangible and coherent. I chose the latter and hope I am able to provide something close to my intent.

In terms of writing this book, the "something" I am supposed to know about is the generation that faces me each day in my classroom. It is the same generation that wanders through streets looking down at their screens or whose laps are aglow in my classroom when the lights are down, while I am teaching.

Second, after nearly four decades of working with teenagers, I have seen a few changes occur in students. I saw these changes in my own children, who both are adult millennials. This leads me, then, to the next reason I wrote this book. Parents began asking me over the past few years, "What is wrong with my child? He won't talk to me anymore, and he is always distracted. He never used to be like that."

The problems with children and technology are looming large for Gen Z. They were never more real for me than when a teenage girl was killed one day while walking to school. She was budded and plugged in, walked across a road, outside the crosswalk, in front of a car. She was struck and killed by a teacher at the school she attended. The answers to what is wrong with our children is a major reason I wrote this book. As you will read, the reasons are many; and many reasons addressed in this book are unique to Gen Z.

Third, I wrote this book for parents to explain what is happening in the brains of their children in this 24/7 era of twenty-first-century digital connectivity. Don't look now, but we are responsible for many of the problems today. We gave our Gen Z children devices to keep them occupied and connected, and now their future is in jeopardy due to their apparent addiction to smart devices and the Internet. Parents must partner with their children's schools, faith communities, and civic organizations to wean them from the very thing we provided them. Gen Z is our product, a unique one at that.

THE UNIQUENESS OF GEN Z

Gen Z is unique. Somewhere around 1995, and up to about 2010, children were born into a world that could never fathom a time before cell phones or the Internet. They have overdeveloped thumbs and tech-neck. Their slouches are prominent, their eyes are sleep deprived, and they are transfixed daily on digital screens. As a generation, they are a corporate perplexity.

Gen Z desires close relationships in the flesh, yet are quite unable to navigate this closeness and leave the digital realm behind to deepen them. They view their devices as parts of their lives, and, in many cases, awaken at night to get their fixes. Smartphones are almost as essential as food and water. In fact, while playing games online, Gen Z children would deprive themselves of food just to remain connected online.

Gen Z is unique for another reason. They have been convinced that emotions are the test of reality and truth. They do this in the most subjective of ways. They are easily offended and hurt for others even when they do not hurt for themselves.

The real world awaits Gen Z. The first Gen Z college graduates already have tasted the fruits of the real world. Some have enrolled in graduate schools. Others have entered the workforce, even begun businesses as entrepreneurs. Gen Z loves entrepreneurship. However, as of 2017, some remain parked in their mothers' basements.

Soon, millions upon millions of hunched-over, easily offended, safe-space, tech-addicted minions will be milling about, seeking work, and carving out their own economic realities. Those who can find the patience to train as teachers may be in for a rude awakening. They might have to put down their cell phones and talk to people. However, if they do not like what they have chosen for employment, they will just walk away and find something else.

Parents, your Gen Z children are unique. They are the first generation to have both *helicopter parents* and *bulldozer parents*. They have been bailed out, excused, and covered for when they desire to do their own thing. Life's hardships and dilemmas have not yet befallen them as a generation. In fact, Gen Z even have all of the same trophies and ribbons for showing up to school, participating in competitions, or athletic events. They are highly decorated, as are all of their friends.

INSPIRATION FOR THIS BOOK

The inspiration for this book came from the students, who have endured my silly personality and corny jokes—some of which have spilled over onto these pages. Over the years my students have made me laugh, made me cry, caused me to pray a lot for them and their families, and we learned together how to grow as teacher and students. Gen Z, however, holds an extra special place in my heart. Their tenderness as people may be derided by many nicknames, most of which are included in this book, but their open hearts and pliable spirits are second-to-none.

Over the years I have had the privilege of working at several Christian schools in Los Angeles, Orange and Kern Counties, in California. Stockdale Christian School, in Bakersfield, still holds a warm place in my heart. I have also served in the Fruitvale School District and Kern High School District; the latter I am blessed to call my place of employment for nearly two decades.

Thousands of students and families have touched my life in immeasurable ways. I am grateful to have had the opportunity to make a difference in so many lives. However, my life has been impacted exponentially, so much more than I could have ever impacted any student entrusted to my tutelage and pedagogy. So, to all of my students, current and former, I cherish all of you and the memories we made, and I thank you from the bottom of my heart. God bless you all.

OK, now where's my coffee?

1
Gen Z Parents

. . . from twenty onwards, the parent's role increasingly becomes to act as mentor, rather than parent.[1]

The King will answer and say to them, "Truly I say to you, to the extent that you did it to one of these brothers of Mine, even the least of them, you did it to Me."[2]

Inventor Thomas Edison failed in his experiments hundreds to thousands of times. Former National Basketball Association great Michael Jordan was once cut from his high school basketball team. Legendary UCLA basketball coach John Wooden missed the final shot in a championship game as a youth. Albert Einstein did not speak for several years after his birth. Stories like these, and so many others, have at least one thing in common: people fail.

People's failures and shortcomings help to shape them. Disappointments along the way should not diminish their ultimate drive for success. As a young man seeking funding, Edison was laughed at and told he was too eccentric. As a teenager, Jordan had no idea he would ever make his high school team. Wooden thought he let down his team by losing the championship. Einstein was thought to have learning disabilities. Failure can be a road sign pointing toward success.

Many Gen Z parents have one thing in common that may not result in their children's ultimate success. They step in to minimize their children's failure. In so doing, Gen Z children miss some of life's biggest learning moments; as a result, they are not prone to demonstrate resilience and an overcoming nature. Failure is an option for children, and choosing it regularly is not the best option. But this failure does not mean they are failures at life, or failures as people. Parents should monitor their children's choices and allow them to grow into making more mature and solid choices over time.

Parents who do not allow their children to experience failure are not allowing them to develop character traits such as humility, perseverance, dedication, and self-control necessary for a balanced adulthood. Gen Z parents must fight the tendency to think that their children's failures mean they are bad parents. They are not. Good parenting is not bailing out children or making certain outcomes on their behalf fit the parents' liking. Good parenting, in this sense, is not perfect parenting. Perfect parenting does not exist. But good parents know what is best for their children and allow them the same opportunity to grow in their decision making according to their own set of choices.[3]

Shaping Decisions

Helping to shape a child away from making poor decisions is far better than stepping in to make certain their decisions are not expressed. Parents must be on guard to avoid being swept up in defining their own success through their children. Likewise, bailing out children sets an expectation and a precedent for the parent to uphold.

Many parents have experienced their child's sweet-talking. These parents understand this cajoling as manipulation, which often comes packaged with begging and whining—especially when children observe something they desire. After denying their child's request, do most parents give in to their tantrum-filled child? Every parent could write his or her own book on child rearing, as common experiences seem to come with the territory for most parents.

Parents of every generation struggle to understand their children. Certain changes occur when children enter the teenage years. The gap of understanding between teenager and parent seems to grow. The gap widens further between generations because of experiences, age differences, interests, and the minds and emotions of teenagers. One reason for this is that children begin to form their own opinions and seek to build their own personhood.

A defining characteristic that adds real challenges to the relationships between parents and children is the widening gap, especially during their youth. This gap is exacerbated by parents' own experiences and their memories of these experiences. For example, children can become more complicated and less communicative as they mature. Parents recall their own youth, summoning memories they have laid in their own parents' minds. Teenage memories can be short on recall. Therefore, there is an experience gap as it relates to the memories established in teenagers' minds and the minds of their parents. What are some other traits and characteristics of these Gen Z parents?

CHARACTERISTICS OF GEN Z PARENTS

No two parents are alike, and no one style of parenting works with all students across every generation. Generation Z parents struggle with many of the same issues as parents of previous generations. Even so, every child is unique, and what works with one child may not necessarily work with another.

One of the more interesting aspects of raising children is the perception they have of themselves. Being young means they have little or no historical frame of reference. As a result, each generation of children maintains a general, exclusive persona, which causes them to believe they are different from every other generation of children. Conversely, parents of Gen Z children recall how they were raised and then apply a similar approach to today's children. This reinforces the axiom *Our parents did a decent job, and we didn't turn out so bad!* But generational parenting styles have clear differences.

Some Parenting Differences

For example, baby boomers' parents characteristically are reserved. Their parenting style is considered more silent. Challenging parental authority usually resulted in some form of discipline, often physical in nature, resembling the way they were disciplined. Children often were told to be seen and not heard "if they knew what was good for them." The children of the boomers, those who comprise Gen X and even Gen Y, often found their upbringing less harsh and more engaging on verbal levels. Questioning methods of discipline began with the Dr. Spock and his influence and impact in the 1960s and 1970s. The difference between the attention paid to boomers by their parents, and the attention paid to boomers' children is like night and day.

Parents today seem much more verbal, especially in telling their children how much they love them. This love is also taken a step farther, often enough, by purchasing goods. Earning these goods today appears secondary to children; automobiles, motorcycles, and recreational vehicles are sometimes purchased for children as gifts.

"Cool" parents throw parties for older children, have sleepovers, rent motor homes and take trips, and they are not shy about having their children miss school for vacation. Older students cut classes, miss college, and go away with friends. When parents today decide to take their children out for vacation, schools are left to understand and make concessions for the families.

In today's entitlement-minded America, parents of older children, especially high school age students, willingly phone their child's school to excuse her for a day at the beach. On some level, making excuses for a child's behavior is disturbing. Parents are teaching children the wrong message by practicing "feel-good moments." Personal anecdotes abound of Gen Z parents excusing student-athletes from school on games days, to go out with friends for lunch, or even stay home and rest.

Stories from attendance offices relate how parents think children need time off from school and from the stress of daily living, in much the same way adults say they need time off from work. Parents simply expect teachers and schools to understand that their children are under a lot of pressure. Therefore, if parents choose to excuse their child's cut from one or two classes, because they were up late, or attended a concert—or because a group of students wants to get together for a few hours at one student's home—then everyone should just understand.

Gen Z parents have created a monster with school tardies, cuts, and excuses for their children. They know that little can be done to them in the process. Herein lie vast differences in the generations. Parents of previous generations were not so quick to bail out a child who forgot a lunch at home. In the old-school philosophy of child rearing, if a child went hungry for a day, because he forgot to bring his lunch to school, then the next day he might remember. In the new method of bailing out children, Gen Z parents rush out and buy lunch and hand deliver it to their child. The parent becomes hero for a day. Certainly, not all Gen Z parents fall under this characterization. But Gen Z's entitlement expectations come from somewhere.

Work ethic was very different in previous generations, and excuses were not the norm. Responsibility was taken more seriously. When Gen Z parents show their children how to fabricate reality to massage circumstances in their favor, outcomes become the foundations upon which ethics are built.

Gen Z children did not create their own sets of behaviors in a vacuum. Gen Xers and millennials are the parents of the Z generation. What they see and learn often is how they will come to act. Previous generations invented most of the technology we have at our fingertips today, and certainly there is enough finger pointing to go around.

Gen Z is the group that identifies its own generation by the possession and use of that technology. Gen Z is also a consequence of its parents, who have been characterized by the three unflattering general terms addressed next.

THREE GENERAL TYPES OF GEN Z PARENTS

As most are aware, children are reflections of parents and often demonstrate these reflections in a variety of ways. The adoption of parents' values, whether political ideologies, particular familial axiomatic phrases, or a sense of humor, are what elicit friends' and other family members' comments about how much a child is like his father or mother.

The inescapable fact remains that not only do children reflect parents in many ways, but parents affect children in myriad ways. These effects are the result of direct training, discipline, and consistent application of expectations and behaviors. Sometimes the results bring joy. Other times, the results are disappointing, and it's back to the drawing board to try things another way. Parental effects usually are observed in schools across patterns of behavior, which include choices of friends and activities. Therefore, it is important to examine and assess the types of parenting for nearly fifty million Gen Z children.

Three general types of parenting are addressed in the following sections: *overly aggressive, uncompromising, and controlling; tolerant, disengaged, and distant;* and *even-keel, informed.* Each of these three general types of Gen Z parents has been assigned nicknames, which are discussed as well.

Gen Z Helicopter-Bulldozer Parents

Aggressive and highly competitive parents usually are heavily involved in their children's lives. They practice regular communication with schools, sometimes over minuscule issues. They are heavy-handed in the selection of their children's teachers, classes, clubs, and sports. This type of parenting crosses all generations and has been a hallmark of the energetic and control-type parents for as long as anyone can remember. Baby boomers remember the constant reminders to phone parents upon arrival at friends' homes, as well as upon leaving to return home.

Some baby boomer requirements carried over into Generation X, as well as to the millennials. Each still had to contend with reminders to stay in touch with parents. However, these later generations now had access to technology to ease the parent concerns and provide immediate peace of mind.

The technological advancement was a panacea for the controlling parents, under the guise of safety, as well as satisfying the parental penchant for involvement and control. The reader should ask whether the technology produced the controlling parent, or whether parents were controlling beforehand but it became more pronounced as a result of the technology.

Continuous-Access Generation. Gen Z parents have come to expect continuous access to their children. Working parents celebrate the fact that they can contact their child at any moment, even during school. Some Gen Z parents forget that they are interrupting classroom time. Sometimes one person's control diminishes the control of another, which is often the effect on teachers. Today's parents and their children can be viewed by previous generations as one continuous-access generation.

Americans have only to reflect on the April 20, 1999, Columbine tragedy to understand parents' need to have immediate access to their students. Extreme incidents like these are always in the psyche of those with school-age children. Those born in and around this date now comprise the teenagers and young adults of Gen Z—some who might have children of their own.

Parental control over and against their child's education is one thing. Interrupting another professional at work—namely, the teacher—is another. Parents who resort to immediate gratification of offspring contact, or hustle to provide a lunch for a forgetful child, often disregard that their actions would never be tolerated in most other workplace environments.[4]

Parents should consider another factor. Cell phones can have negative effects during alarming situations and can create more harm than good at school and in their children's classrooms. Imagine that during an emergency all first-responder services are kept at bay because of students' and parents' phone calls and texts in the thousands being sent from one location. Lives could be placed in jeopardy. Just the mention of this probably elevated emotional awareness or anxiety levels of Gen Z parents. Anyone seeking to reverse the tide of cell phone addiction on school campuses would have a better chance of putting the proverbial toothpaste back into its tube.

Immediate Distractions

Consider another issue: the empowerment and enablement of parents and students to have immediate access to each other. This brings with it many distractions, with which teachers now have to contend. Countless teachers have heard the impassioned phrases, "I have to text my mom back right now," or "I have to have my dad bring my lunch."

The ubiquity of technology often is seen as a dream for parents with tight controls over their Gen Z students. The students, however, sometimes view this quite differently. Parents of Gen Z students want answers now and are insecure about not having all of the facts and details to appease their curiosity and bolster emotional investment. Lengthy e-mails and immediate social media posts characterize many Gen Z parents' actions. A new phrase can apply to this newest sense of connectedness: *immediate gratification on steroids.*

Hovering. Parents of Gen Z students hover over their children's whereabouts and activities. Hence they have been given the name "helicopter parents" by those who study their actions, interactions, and oversight of minutiae. Parents who schedule and then monitor their children's daily activities are equally involved in academics at school. The same can be said for helicopter parents in terms of athletics.

With respect to competition, the parental cry of "unfair and foul" often comes from picturing their child's athletic scholarship from a university slipping away. Sometimes a lack of playing time in games brings parental aggressiveness to its highest levels. As a former coach for many years, it has become obvious that parents are the true competitors, and their children often are the participants in the parents' competitions. Aggressive, hovering parents are certain to find ways to benefit their children, but at what cost? In addition, what have the children learned?

For example, a high school teacher, volunteering to coach a fifth-grade basketball team, recently was threatened by a father who approached him from the stands in front of other parents. Rather than get into a physical altercation with the father, the coach "handed him the ball and walked away."[5] The teacher-coach was reprimanded by the administration for leaving the team unsupervised. The teacher-coach had feared for his safety,[6] given the proximity of the whirring helicopter blades.

The Lack of Tact. Another issue is at stake here with overly aggressive parents: the lack of tact. One person's perceived communication urgency does not necessarily carry the same urgency with others. Whether in e-mail, voicemail, or in person, unfiltered words can result in a lack of tact. What may be more important to a parent is to win at all cost on behalf of her child; this may be the driver for Gen Z parent aggressiveness.

Game of Gotcha!

Today's Gen Z students, from elementary through high school, are quick to pull out their cell phones and text their parents as if in a game of tactless "gotcha" with the teacher or those in authority. When feelings are hurt, parents are told. When an exam score is not to the students' liking, or when students feel they are not treated fairly, cell phones are pinging. Teachers across the nation are subject to classroom phone calls directly from parents, sometimes within seconds of the initial contact. E-mails are sent requesting immediate attention as to why something occurred with their child.

Any interruption takes away from the learning environment. Some interruptions go deeper and harm relationships in the classroom, causing rifts between the teacher and parent. Parents need to understand this: When a student is armed with a smartphone, the moment he perceives hurt in any way, communication is sent to make him feel better, impulsively punish someone in retaliation, or hold the teacher accountable for something viewed as unfair. Parents must suppress their desire for immediate answers to emotional reactions by their children.

Hyper-Parent Involvement. Hyper-parents are those in the stands at games yelling at the referees. They call attention to themselves and sometimes get into confrontations during and after their children's games. The roar of hovering hyper-parents can be deafening. This is taking aggressiveness to an entirely new level. What is worse, the aggressiveness can become ugly and abusive in short order. An emotional situation that escalates by involving peers is a form of *group dump*.

There are explanations as to why Gen Z parents are keen on hyper-involvement with their children. One major reason is that the parents are in the prime of their lives, and their age group is one of the most highly involved in day-to-day matters economically. Gen Z parents often are overlooked, because many of the parents with Gen Z children belong to Gen X. In other words, Gen Z parents are "smack dab in the middle innings of life, which tend to be short on drama and scant of theme . . . bookended by two much larger generations . . . Gen-Xers are a low-slung, straight-line bridge between two noisy behemoths."[7]

Some helicopter parents have decided to land, and this group has begun to earn another moniker. The goal for this newer group is to score points on behalf of their children. Parents who now press forward and must win at all cost may now be considered *bulldozer parents*. Parents previously hovered over their children and made certain things worked in their favor, or bailed them out of difficult situations; some now have transitioned to a firmer, authoritarian approach.

When bulldozer parents finish driving home their points, little is left standing between people. Not only are these parents able to get their way, but they plow over anyone who stands in their way. Bulldozer parents are a win-at-all-cost group. For example, bulldozer parents have no problem avoiding the teacher and going directly to the superintendent's office, or even the media, in order to win a battle. The main objective is to go big and step over anyone and anything in their way in order to win. Bulldozer parents are the least respected on school campuses.

With the ubiquity of cell phones today, and children quick to inform parents of every little happening, the issue of control has notched upward. Bulldozer parents' actions incite their own children to action through technology and continuous connections they provide.

Gen Z Distant-Frenzied and Enabling Parents

The distant-frenzied parent is different from the hyper-involved aggressive parent. Unlike the helicopter and bulldozer parents, the distant-frenzied parent appears to remain in the background until enough moments are strung together to cause concern. Whether by self-control, procrastination, or just plain old busyness of life, the distant-frenzied parent resorts to compiling circumstances resulting in explosive emotional outbursts. Rather than regular aggressiveness, distant-frenzied parent passivity is enabling: some children know how far to go before an emotional reaction occurs. In a larger sense, distant-frenzied parents are characterized by extreme moments of panic.

Those moments usually arise when children keep them in the dark about school and grades. The panic often results as frustration levels build due to parents' inconsistency in monitoring their children's grades. Most everyone feels the result of this panic, and teachers recognize the e-mails and phone calls that are the outcome. The panic usually comes at the end of an academic term and the week prior to grades closing, normally a parent's first contact with his or her child's teacher. The first question is what can my child do to make up all the missing work.

No New Is Good News

Distant-frenzied parents relish the axiom that "no news is good news." They trust—that is, until they hear something that proves this axiom invalid. Last-minute panic breaks loose when distant-frenzied parents discover something on their Gen Z student's cell phone, or when they are informed that their child is failing a class or even had not been attending school. Administrators, teachers, and coaches usually hear from these parents when they are at emotionally explosive levels. These parents seek is to solve a problem as quickly as possible, even one that might have been brewing for weeks.

The Even-Keel Informed Parents

Gen Z parents who stay informed, view controversy as part of life, and deal with it appropriately and tactfully develop the best relationships with teachers. They also stand the greatest chance of staying connected to their children in healthy ways throughout the teenage years. These parents do not thrive on controversy. They have no vendetta and practice no assertive vindictiveness on behalf of something deemed unfair to their child. On a school-related note, the avoidance of unnecessary conflict enables learning to continue in the classroom and the development of a deeper parent-teacher relationship that benefits the children. These are the even-keel parents.

Informed parents make it their business to monitor most of what their children do, and they are quite attentive toward that end. They are informed about their children's academics, often communicating with teachers without anyone else knowing about their communications. It is the way they go about being informed that keeps their children in the middle, holding them accountable both at home and at school. Active and informed parenting is not motivated to draw attention to itself. For the most part, parents who are actively informed secure knowledge and information without great fanfare. This type of parenting is issue oriented.

As Gen Z begins to have families of their own, it will be most interesting to observe whether they develop their own form of parenting or adopt their parents' form. Pendulums are meant to swing. Generations are good examples of pendulums, especially concerning methods of child rearing. A new technological paradigm exists to challenge Gen Z, and it is not going away anytime soon. Parents can be certain that smart technologies will play roles in the upbringing of at least the next generation of children.

SCHOOL ANECDOTES

As all teachers are aware, some of the most bizarre occurrences find their way into school classrooms. Sometimes these eyebrow-raising experiences come by way of student description and explanation. Other times, statements are made by children and their parents orally or by written communication.

As many teachers in elementary and middle schools can attest, some of the stories that go home are quite flabbergasting. Parents, certainly, drop their jaw in wonderment and disbelief. Students take home some of the most interesting stories about what transpired throughout the school day. The younger the student, the more obtuse the stories can seem. Whatever the age, Gen Z students have little self-regulation when they use their communication devices, and parents usually are in the loop very quickly.

As previously noted, students now text their parents seconds after a classroom event. They post on Twitter exactly what goes on at every moment of their lives. If an incident is not interpreted correctly, emotion added to secondary issues can result in the misreading of a message. Veteran teachers who have been online for nearly twenty years are well aware of the inability to read emotion and body language in a post or text message. Attempts to do so are inconsistent at best. This is one reason Snapchat and other video recording and imaging are of greater importance to Gen Z. That which is closest to real time and life is enthralling, if not epic.

Most teachers have their own anecdotes about students, and most parents have their own about school incidents. Recently, *Good Housekeeping* magazine published some of the crazier things teachers claim were said to them by parents of their students. Some of the anecdotes described here originally were found on several Reddit threads.[8]

To begin, a frustrated and exhausted parent told a teacher that while her son was at school, he was the teacher's problem and not the parent's. Next, when a problem arose on an elementary school campus, a parent accused teachers of unprofessionalism because they did not know the names of every child at the school.[9] Rumors spread around the community about how the school her children attended hires only uncaring teachers.

Stories such as these take on very interesting twists, often attracting peculiar responses after the stories are shared. For example, a father claimed his son was only dumb at school, not while at home. The implication is that attending school makes kids dumber. Parents sometimes argue and even fight over grades. These types of parents also think teachers play favorites with children, but they are all right with this as long as their child is one of the favorites.

Some parents defend plagiarism by claiming that intellectual property posted online, copied and pasted by their children, is just fine because such property rights have gray areas. Add these to the criticisms of teachers for teaching "the normal kid," while others have it more difficult because they have to deal with greater difficulties in the classroom teaching *abnormal* kids. What can a teacher do upon hearing such things but smile?

Some parents proclaim their dislike of the "unhealthy" school lunches while supplying Starbucks' and McDonald's foods and drinks as alternatives. One of the more interesting anecdotes from the Reddit article is found in the demands of one hyper-aggressive parent who required all parent-teacher correspondence to be notarized so that the communication was official. Dare it be said that trust issues were involved?[10] Technology makes incidents such as these as shareable as they are observable, which is why Gen Z parents must not overreact on behalf of their children when the children contact by them via text message. Having all of the facts is best with any generation, especially Gen Z.

GEN Z PARENTS AS ALLIES IN THE CLASSROOM

Understanding parenting styles is all well and good. Being acutely aware of teaching styles is equally beneficial. Yet, without making allies of the two, there cannot be a meeting of the minds and hearts necessary to work together to lead young people into their futures. Therefore, teachers should make regular attempts to understand the personalities and dynamics that go into the makeup of the families and the things they value. Parents should connect with a similar goal in mind.

Teachers have the opportunity to tap into the skills of their students' parents. If handled properly, the dynamics in the classroom are enhanced by parental advocacy and assistance. The strengths of parents can help to deepen the professional relationships between home and school. In order to achieve this, Gen Z parents would do well to reflect on some of the strengths and weaknesses of parenting styles.

When parents become involved in schools, some of these styles find their way into classrooms. As with other generations, Gen Z parents demonstrate certain styles that can make a difference in children's lives in education. Teachers should strive to consider how to incorporate each of these attributes into their classrooms in positive ways, as they partner with parents for the benefit of the children and families involved.

Parental Strengths Are a Plus

Gen Z parents whose strengths are found in aggressiveness and control, who are relentlessly motivated toward achievement, can be real assets to teachers. The same is true for parents whose parenting style is actively informed, or frenzied and much more passive. Each style can be shaped toward excellent outcomes for schools and classrooms. Involving parents is a necessary component for classroom success, and parental involvement is crucial for the success of any school.

Parenting styles can be allied toward success in the classroom in assuming leadership roles as fund-raisers and trip organizers, helping in athletic and academic competitions and events, and others. These take master organization to accomplish. Parents can assist and run school awards ceremonies, design and develop community outreach service for students, help to write and edit a school or classroom newsletter, monitor and enhance a class website, volunteer in classrooms, and assist at other parent group activities and events.

Some of these activities mesh with high-energy, gregarious parents seeking to be in charge and take command. Others can easily use parents whose styles are more amenable to supporting from the background, or assisting with the logistics of events. Gen Z parents need to step forward to help offset the time constraints today's teachers face.

Teachers should be wary of placing individualists in charge of other parents, if they evidence an inability to work together, lack necessary tact for communicating, view issues competitively, or have a tendency to hurt others with insensitive words. Teachers must get to know the students' parents if they expect to become allies while working together for Gen Z.

FORMING MEANINGFUL RELATIONSHIPS
BETWEEN GEN Z AND THEIR PARENTS

The majority of Gen Z students learned about swiping debit and credit cards long before they could stand up and walk. "Computer screens and smart phones were always a part of their lives. Parents shared their first birthdays, first steps, and first words over blogs, Twitter, Facebook, and Instagram. They have laptops in elementary school. They use Google Drive for homework assignments and apps on their smart devices. They make online friends around the world on video games and social networks."[11] Forming meaningful relationships can begin by inviting parents to share their expertise with their children's classes.

Most Gen Z students share one constant with every generation of students that preceded them: friends are very important. What is also important is the priority Gen Z places on their devices. Often parent involvement in a class is very impressive to a child's friends. To Gen Z, a tech-savvy parent is a winning parent.

Even as these things are true, surveys indicate that of much greater importance to Gen Z children are their families. Families offer Gen Z children things that friends cannot. Gen Z parents are to be lauded, and their value is never to be underestimated. Technology can never be a replacement for the human element and love afforded children of Gen Z.

Five Key Elements for Deeper Relationships

In forming relationships with their children, parents can support five key elements toward deepening their relationships with their children. The temptation for Gen Z parents today is to think that communicating through social media and texting can replace face-to-face conversation, hugs, and eye contact. It is incorrect to think that a digital presence brings with it the same reality as a physical presence. Although Gen Z tends to believe these are synonymous, there is no genuine substitute for human interaction. If left unchecked, Gen Z is all technology, all day. That being the case, despite all denials, Gen Z children "really do want face-to-face"[12] communication with their parents.

The five elements that benefit parents and children of Gen Z are (1) unconditional parental and familial acceptance; (2) validation of Gen Z individuality and personhood; (3) parental wisdom that goes beyond 140 characters, memes, or emojis; (4) personal experiences grounded in real interpersonal relationships, which occur by (5) spending "real" time together, to develop deeper commitments to each other. Digital is "real time." Gen Z ultimately prefers "real life."

Parental and Familial Unconditional Acceptance. Gen Z is compelled to see themselves on social media and to elicit reactions. Often their acceptance is limited to "likes" by online friends, casual acquaintances, and complete strangers. Validation and acknowledgment by friends online do not replace parental and familial acceptance. Parents love their children when they look their best, look their worst, have good days and bad. Unconditional acceptance is based on who children are as people, not on what they do to please others or some digital creation.

A note of caution here to Gen Z parents: friends often are an excellent source of support for Gen Z. But these same friends can be sources of great angst. The digital realm brings with it many more opportunities for people to affect emotions. It is a double-edged sword for Gen Z. On the one hand, the digital realm enables sensations that can lead to emotional highs. On the other hand, these highs can be diminished with clicks of various levels of "like" buttons.

Parents have the ability to make the world real again and to demonstrate that, although the digital world can reach one's emotions and affect states of mind, it cannot accept people unconditionally. It simply has no will. Someone, somewhere, always will demonstrate an affinity toward harm intentionally, manipulating a photo for laughs, even bullying. Not all emotions experienced by Gen Z in their world of digital devices and Internet access are peace and love.

Validation of Individuality and Personhood. Gen Z has to take precautions so as not to get their value from their online experiences. "Fish-lips," cute poses, exposure of one's body, and muscle pictures get reactions. However, images such as these are not who people are: posting is what they do for reactions. Confusing online personhood with imagery is best exposed in "catfishing," the perception that someone is being honest and open online, that their photos are genuine, and that their identity is trustworthy. When a person is "catfished," the opposite of the online expectation is usually the result.

A tragic event occurred while I was writing this chapter. A divorced grandmother of millennials with Gen Z children, took her own life. The mixture of sharing her life online, showing only sexy and model-like photos of herself, and entertaining a public persona, covered the true issues that plagued her. If one were only to look at the photos and written posts online, the image put forward was of a person with a perfect life. The reality was far from it. Her imagery became her online reality, which ultimately led to her suicide. The image portrayed could cover her true identity for only so long. Once again, one's personhood is not to be defined by the digital world. Life and death issues are real, and they are so much more important than photographs manipulated or numbers of "likes." Gen Z must be taught that they are people who have special value to us all. Investing in personhood is vastly more important than counting followers. Gen Z parents would do well to understand that their children's identities cannot be truly realized in a number of online "followers."

Parental Wisdom. Any person seeking wisdom from social media sources needs to view life from other angles. The Internet is not necessarily the trusted source for information and facts about how to live, let alone raise children. Recent stories about "fake news" should put this in perspective. There is wisdom that goes beyond 140 characters, cute memes with captions, or emojis that express one's feelings at a particular moment. However, there are some excellent professional parenting sources online, which help to answer questions for parents struggling with Gen Z children. An Internet search can reveal a bounty of organizations, some of which include advice and wisdom collected from parents across the globe.

Gen Z parents are encouraged to take the lead in the cultural battle for the attention of the children and families. American culture would have us believe that recording one's sexual exploits and posting them online is good for one's career, or one's popularity. Culture would also have us believe that masses of people are struggling with sexual identity, that major moral and legal adjustments are necessary and must be accepted as new norms. Truth be told, the media sometimes reveal biases. Political and cultural agendas are not the places for wisdom and truth, to be sure. But they are places for emotion.

At times, parents are wrapped in good intentions, making certain their children have enough experiences to apply to college or have career choices to their liking. But has anyone met a parent who has stated publicly that he is supportive of his child's future career in the adult movie industry, or as a prostitute, or in any other glamorized vice industry? Culture can present itself as casual and attractive. However, parents need to know how culturally acceptable distortions are communicated as truth. The real wisdom of parenting does not come from the streets, nor does true education. So, where does this leave the average Gen Z parent?

Parents of Gen Z children have a wealth of experience to share with their children. It comes from honoring and adhering to previous generations' wisdom and established moral frameworks of right and wrong. Add these to a healthy upbringing and accurate self-perception, complete with choices and consequences, and parents have an excellent chance to provide Gen Z with the direction they need.

However, parents first have to get their children to put down their cell phones and pull out their earbuds in order for them to hear this wisdom. Parents also have to unplug themselves. Relationships are more than living arrangements and meeting of needs with provisions of technology and money. Wisdom can only be passed along if people take time to share it and apply it.

The Value of Personal Experience. One of the more attractive features of Gen Z parents is that they tend to be grounded in reality. Like parents of other generations, some of the shortcomings and poorer choices made are not readily or easily discussed among family members. However, the parents of Gen Z children are more apt to use their own life experiences toward shaping the decisions they intend their children to make. Parents' personal experiences lend credibility to their words and opinions, bringing with them an aura of expertise and respectability.

Parents of Gen Z students also know that if they can keep those children busy, they will have less opportunity to find trouble or make some of the same decisions as their parents. In one way, technology has worked as an advantage. Personal experience is a good teacher, and it can best be communicated by demonstrating genuineness and empathy. This leads to the last element beneficial to Gen Z.

Spending Real Time Together. Family relationships are multidimensional; with the constant presence of technology, spending time together as a family might come as a challenge. How many meals have been spent with children's earbuds plugging their ears? What parent today has not told their children to put down their phones and pay attention?

In the midst of today's generational challenges, some constants remain. One of these is spending time together as a family. Some families do not have the luxury of regular vacations, due to financial or schedule constraints. Whether through family meals or athletics, youth group meetings, rushing to piano lessons, soccer, or gymnastics classes, Gen Z parents know the value of being involved in their children's lives. But does involvement with activities equate to being "present" with their children? Gen Z parents would do well to reflect on whether shuttling children from event to event is a distraction from spending real time together, as eating fast food on the way to piano lessons or soccer precludes a family meal.

Past generations had their distractions and annoyances. Which previous generation cannot recall the echoing refrain of "turn down that stereo!"? Whatever the generation, the catch is to work with and through the technological distractions.

Gen Z is automating its own behaviors. It is learning to replace *face to face* with *head down*, staring into a screen to find ways to relate. Because there is no physical presence between people who use technological communication, there can be no real intimacy. The façade that is built around things digital is based on perception, anticipation, and emotion—many times irreconcilably so.

Children of Gen Z need physical affection from their parents, as did each preceding generation. Stories abound of children who resort to touching monitors that capture the face of a parent who is deployed in the military. Facetime and Skype are no substitutes for hugs and loving touches. Gen Z may believe they are getting used to technological relationships, but spending real time together cannot be replaced by digital time.

Along with families, schools and teachers offer extended familial relationships. Where the family has been fractured by divorce, or there are single-parent households, schools often are the stopgap for these Gen Z students and their families. To the extent that schools are finding Gen Z issues unique, they come with their own strengths and weaknesses, concerns and critics. These are addressed in detail in my second book in this series, *The Entitled Generation: Helping Teachers Teach and Reach the Minds and Hearts of Generation Z*.

GEN Z PARENTS' SURVEY

Three hundred sixty-one Gen Z parents were surveyed to gain additional insight into the details of the relationships and understanding of Gen Z children. Ten items were asked of Gen Z parents; the questions and results are included next.

1. *Between what ranges of years was at least one of your children born?*

   The majority of parents surveyed (39 percent) stated that at least one of their children was born between 1995 and 2000. The second-most responses, about 22 percent, indicated they had at least one child born between 2006 and 2010.

   The years 2001–2005 had 17 percent of respondents, and 1990–1994 and 2011–2016 were tied in responses with 11 percent each. Parents could check as many ranges as necessary, and each response was counted as separate for the data collection.

2. *If your child is disciplined for something that occurred during the school day, how would you deal with this situation?*

   The supermajority, 83 percent of parents, stated they would take the word of both their child and the teacher because, in their view, there is always more than one side to a story. Not one parent said he would take his child's word "only" for what occurred, foremost because their child does not lie. Another 11 percent said they would take the word of the teacher, because the teacher is the adult, whereas only 6 percent would contact the principal directly to deal with the situation, bypassing the teacher.

3. *What method of contacting/corresponding with your children's teachers do you prefer?*

   A clear majority of parent respondents (53 percent) replied they would use written communication, including notes and e-mail, to communicate with their Gen Z child's teacher. A little less than one-third (31 percent) preferred face-to-face discussions, or conferences with their child's teacher. Phone contacts, either directly or through voicemail messages (11 percent) and online messaging, including cell phone texting (6 percent), had the fewest responses.

4. *Select a region of the nation that most closely represents where you reside.*

   Sixty-four percent of the parent respondents replied that their residence was in the West. Eleven percent of the Gen Z parents were in the Southwest United States. The Northeast, Midwest, and Southeast regions each had just over 8 percent.

5. *Have you ever bypassed your child's teacher or professor to speak directly to an administrator at school/college, on behalf of your Gen Z child?*

   Only three of eight answer possibilities were selected as responses by parents. Approximately 61 percent of Gen Z parents stated that they did not bypass their child's teacher or professor to talk directly to an administrator on behalf of their child. Thirty-three percent said they had bypassed their child's teacher, but not their professor. Approximately 6 percent claimed they practice this regularly, sometimes multiple times per week.

6. *How would you rate your child's access and use of smartphone technology and the Internet?*

   Fifty-eight percent of parents said their Gen Z child's access and use of smartphone technology and the Internet are monitored and under control. An additional 31 percent stated that their Gen Z child is free to use both the smartphone and the Internet as they wish, and that they had no real concern at this time. Another 8 percent were very concerned about the excessive time their child spent on smartphones and the Internet, and worry about addiction. Approximately 3 percent believe their child is already addicted to their devices.

7. *Does your child post on social media sites, such as Instagram, Snapchat, Facebook, Twitter, YouTube, etc.?*

Most parents (50 percent) claimed that their Gen Z child did not post on any social media sites. This was followed by approximately 36 percent who said they were aware their Gen Z child posted occasionally on one or more media sites throughout the day, and just over 11 percent said their Gen Z child posted regularly on one or more social media sites throughout the day. Three percent replied that they had no idea to which social media sites their child posts, or if they post at all.

8. *In what ways outside of school do you think teachers and schools could support Gen Z parents and families?*

Forty-seven percent of parents would support periodic parent nights at school, to explore issues and solutions for problems facing today's families and children. In contrast, 28 percent said it is *no business of the school* how they raise their children and would *not want the school to offer support* to families. Fourteen percent would accept more school-directed social services to families, while 11 percent of parents would support more one-on-one contact with teachers and administrators after school hours.

9. *During regular school hours, how many times do you connect with your child, by texting or phoning?*

An overwhelming 83 percent of parents responded that they do not in any way contact their child during regular school hours. Approximately 8 percent claim to have contact with the Gen Z child between one and three times per day, and another 8 percent said they contact their child as often as they want or need to throughout the school day.

10. *Have you ever sent your child a text message or received one from him or her while he or she was in class?*

Seventy-five percent of parents responded they never have received a text message or phone call from their child while he or she was in class. The remaining 25 percent stated they had received a text message or phone call from their child while he or she was in class.

SUMMARY OF THE SURVEY RESPONSES

Here are some of the highlights of the survey responses from Gen Z parents:

- Some 361 parents responded to the social media survey posted for one week on Facebook, Twitter, and Instagram.

- The majority of parents (39 percent) said at least one of their Gen Z children was born between 1995 and 2000.
- A supermajority of parents (83 percent) stated that in situations where conflict arises at school, they would believe both their child's and the teacher's versions.
- A clear majority of Gen Z parents (53 percent) use written communication as the primary form of communication with their child's teacher.
- The majority of parents (64 percent) responding to the survey live in the West.
- Sixty-one percent of parents said they did not bypass their child's teacher or professor in order to talk directly to an administrator on behalf of their child.
- The majority of Gen Z parents (58 percent) monitor their child's access to technology and the Internet.
- About 50 percent of the parents said their child does not post on any social media sites.
- Forty-seven percent of parents are supportive of periodic parent night at their local schools.
- A supermajority of Gen Z parents (83 percent) do not contact their child through technology during regular school hours.
- Seventy-five percent had never received a text message or phone call from their child while he or she was in class.

Many teachers will read the survey responses by parents and wonder if they are living in the same universe. One of the inside jokes about Gen Z and their communications devices is that they enjoy blaming their parents for contacting them while the students are in class. Some teachers joke that many of their students must have at least five parents, or that the same grandmother passed away for the fourth time.

Considering the number of cell phones and smartphones on school campuses, it is inconceivable that communication will not occur between families. This author is not alone in having answered several students' phones, only to have the parent on the other end of the call. Technology probably is so much a part of our daily routines that sometimes forgetting with whom we communicate is to be expected.

ADVICE FOR GEN Z PARENTS

First, if anything practical is to be shared with parents of Gen Z students, it would be to assume that students know more about their smartphones than parents are aware. Second, make certain they are aware of what their children are posting, with whom they are texting, and with whom they are exchanging videos and photos. Generally, parents should be aware that their Gen Z children use their data mostly for social reasons, less for music and entertainment. Technology is a wonderful tool. This tool can be used for good, and it can be used to hide so much from parents. So, parents beware that today's parenting brings with it the necessity of becoming technologically and digitally literate.

Advice for parents often can be misinterpreted as expertise, when it really is experience. All children are different, and placing them together in a classroom does little to help understand them on any greater level. Parents know their children best, and life's difficulties often provide the crucible through which this knowledge deepens and the family relationships grow. The passage of time brings with it shorter memories of the past, a basic truth to which many parents with adult children can gladly attest. Selective memories enable families often to remember only the good moments of the past. Contrast this relationship reality with virtual and digital perpetuity and ask yourself, "Which is more forgiving and accepting?"

Parents of Gen Z children face some challenges differently than parents of the past. This does not mean that past practices are not still prominent challenges for today's youth. Alcohol and drugs remain constants, as do sex and additional moral and vice concerns. Illicit behaviors today can lead to death, or a sentence to imminent death.

What is meant by different challenges pertains to the ease with which a person's past is accessible via today's digital storage in the Cloud. Revisiting one's youth from the Cloud may have dire personal or career-ending consequences. How many times have we read about someone's past emerging as problematic right at the moment they embark on a new direction or garner public attention? Gen Z parents should be diligent against this on their children's behalf.

Since the advent of ubiquitous communication devices and the Cloud, the ease with which the past is made present is emerging as a new set of norms. Take for example pornography online. This has led to a brand-new addiction affecting possibly millions from Gen Z. Add to this the need for personal attention, narcissism, and the notion of personal entitlement, and the generational challenges quickly take different shapes. What is different about videos posted online is that they can be retrieved on demand, and the rest is history.

NAVIGATING CHOICES AND CONSEQUENCES WITH GEN Z CHILDREN

Drawing lines between right and wrong is becoming more difficult for American families, but draw them they must. Culture always will press the boundaries and present fringes as norms. Families would do well to consider the "voices" within Gen Z's culture that clamor for the very attention of their children. Technology is one of these major voices.

Parents would also do well to steer children away from Gen Z burrowing deeper and deeper into the Internet. This practice is made easier by the addictive elements

and enticements found online. Choices come with consequences. Parental evalua-
tion of distractions and temptations both faced and experienced by Gen Z children
could help to lift the generation to more reflective, critical thinking. However, this
elevation certainly is not accomplished by limiting a person to an online photo-
graph, or 140 characters. Parents must guard against succumbing to the rapid search
for answers as solutions to understand Gen Z. Likewise, the answers to life's questions are not found in clicking on the first Google link. Optimized, speedy Web
traffic does not always lead to optimized, deeper lives.

Slow Them Down

Parents should fight their children's tendency to make impulsive, snap decisions
and settle on the first thing that comes to mind as the solution to some of life's
complicated situations. Life is not about being first and finding the simplest way
to solve an issue. It is more about being certain, being correct, and respected by
others because of wise decisions. Building character takes time and is counter-
intuitive to impulsivity, which is the essence of most of the parental battles with
Gen Z today. Gen Z may not be able to backtrack from its smart technology, but
parents must get them at least to moderate its use in order to relate. This, after
all, is what everyone desires.

Life should be about learning more and more about these better choices and less
and less about peers "voices." There are more people in the Gen Z world than the
group receiving the text message or those tagged on an Instagram or Twitter post.
Watching a Snapchat or doctoring a Facebook photo is fun. But what do these daily
practices do to assist Gen Z in deepening relationships with people? Again, choices
have consequences. One person's fun may lead to unintended consequences.

Refuse to Accept Excuses and Make None for Ourselves

All parents struggle while raising families. Some of the struggles come with
holding children accountable. Placing headphones over children's ears brings
a certain peace to parenting. Once the headphones are removed, the story often
takes a twist. Occupied children make for fewer challenges. The enhanced use
of technology as discipline only means added challenges once the technology is
removed. However, Gen Z must be held accountable for its choices.

Parents should demonstrate how this accountability works. In order for success
moments to occur, Gen Z parents must strive to stop covering for their children's
choices. Gen Z parents can only expect Gen Z children to be as responsible as
this responsibility is demonstrated. Gen Z's digital world is their reality. Parental
guidance today requires parents to know this world. Parents should present reality
to their children as it should be and encourage them to make good choices based
on respect for themselves, the Golden Rule, and because they are taught right
from wrong at home.

Gen Z is becoming a bored generation. This boredom is not due to lack of interest in things. Rather, they are bored because their brains are being overloaded with constant switching between aural and visual stimulation. It is true that living on an exciting edge that becomes commonplace is *boring by distractions*.

Discovering What Works

"Wait until your father gets home!" These words still resonate across the generations. Certainly, one form of communication is yelling, and sadly, the parents of this author's generation were adept at this practice. Just writing these words evokes many memories and emotional reactions. The neighborhood screams and public discipline of children were the norm for many of previous generations. Today, if parents scream, their children probably cannot hear them.

Remember, the brains of most Gen Z children are still developing, and some parts of their brains are not as efficient as they will be once fully developed. For example, the prefrontal cortex develops more slowly than some other parts of the brain, which makes carrying out everyday tasks more of challenge. The prefrontal cortex has to work harder to maintain motivation to accomplish the mundane. Therefore, Gen Z is less likely to be lazy than to be brain tired.[13]

For parents, Gen Z brain development may challenge communication skills. At near exhaustion, one of our children might be having an emotional meltdown requiring extra time to sort out the issues. Gen Z parents have to fight the daily battle of short attention spans and blatant disregard of their wishes. When parents use the language of frustration, such as "Why don't you grow up?," they must remember that this is exactly what the children are doing. Adding even more challenge is the fact that Gen Z thinks multitasking is listening to music in one ear while tuning out parents in the other.

Like children from all previous generations, Gen Z children long to be accepted and to find their way around American culture. Parents can help immensely. Gen Z parents love their children and communicate with them differently than previous generations of parents. Even so, Gen Z parents remain uncertain about better ways to communicate with a generation clinging to such expectation.[14]

So, the work of being a Gen Z parent will never end: *once a Gen Z parent, always a Gen Z parent.* Because this is the case, Gen Z parents can use the technology to their advantage. These advantages will be addressed in chapter 4, along with suggestions for parents to gain more understanding in practice with their Gen Z children.

Coming to Grips

Gen Z parents will have to "come to grips" with reality: parenting has changed. Cultural values have changed. Children today seem to be more "inward looking and lack determination in overcoming life obstacles."[15] Children in many nations, including the United States, also are "brought up by the mass media around them."[16] These realities often are in conflict with families and multiple generations that must contend with the changes. However, children truly "want to know about the world"[17] around them. Here is where parents have to do the hard work of parenting to find the time to tell their Gen Z children the truth.

Parents need not change their values or beliefs—especially today, when culture is clamoring for moral and ethical ambiguity. However, it is incumbent upon all parents to realize that the ways children are reared in the United States, and elsewhere, have changed throughout the generations. "Many families today place more focus on positive reinforcements to ensure good behavior."[18] The days are gone when corporal punishment is status quo. Technology seems to be replacing opportunities to get into trouble. They do so by setting up other challenges for parents, and by offering opportunities to discover "trouble" elsewhere.[19] The essential question at this juncture requires continual reflection: *Does the playing of video games, and being online hours a day, remove some of the potential disciplinary actions, as well as stunt interpersonal relationships of Gen Z?*

CONCLUSION

Today's Gen Z children are often "softer," more emotional, and less likely to demonstrate some of the generational traits of their parents and grandparents.[20] Parenting styles mean a lot when raising Gen Z children. Even so, today's Gen Z children seem to possess a deep desire to "change the world—but not in the usual way."[21] Some of this passion likely is driven by ideologies presented to them while at school. While at home, some parents are able to discuss and temper their children's passions. If left to friends, social media, and the Internet culture, the disconnect between parents and their Gen Z children will continue to grow. Gen Z parents need to step into the digital and personal lives of their children in bold ways.

NOTES

1. Harry Barry and Edna Murphy, *Flagging the Screenager: Guiding Your Child through Adolescence and Young Adulthood* (Dublin, Ireland: Liberties Press, 2014), 55.

2. Matthew 25:40, *The New American Standard Bible.*

3. Chip Ingram, "Let Your Kids Fail," *Focus on the Family Magazine*, April 2007. http://www.focusonthefamily.com/parenting/spiritual-growth-for-kids/let-your-kids-fail. Retrieved December 6, 2016.

4. "Cell Phones and Text Messaging in Schools," *National School Safety and Security Services*, 2016. http://www.schoolsecurity.org/trends/cell-phones-and-text-messaging-in-schools/. Retrieved July 30, 2016.

5. Amy Dickinson, "Ask Amy: Threatened Coach Leaves Kids in Gym," *Washington Post*, August 21, 2016. https://www.washingtonpost.com/lifestyle/style/ask-amy-threat ened-coach-leaves-kids-in-gym/2016/08/15/bc6edb46-5b1a-11e6-831d-0324760ca856_ story.html. Retrieved August 21, 2016.

6. Dickinson, "Ask Amy."

7. Paul Taylor "Generation X: America's Neglected 'Middle Child,'" Pew Research Center, June 5, 2014. http://www.pewresearch.org/fact-tank/2014/06/05/generation-x -americas-neglected-middle-child/. Retrieved June 28, 2016. Cf. Paul Taylor, *The Next America: Boomers, Millennials, and the Looming Generational Showdown* (Philadelphia: Perseus Books, 2015 [2014]).

8. Heather Finn, "Fourteen Teachers Share Their Horror Stories about Their Students' Parents," *Good Housekeeping*, August 3, 2016. http://www.goodhousekeeping.com/life/ a39723/teachers-share-parent-horror-stories/. Retrieved August 3, 2016. For additional anecdotes, see also https://www.reddit.com/r/AskReddit/comments/1781b8/teachers_of_ reddit_what_are_your_worst/ and https://www.reddit.com/r/AskReddit/comments/3rossd/ teachers_of_reddit_whats_the_most_outrageous/.

9. Ibid.

10. Ibid.

11. Aubre Andrus, "Gen Z vs. Gen Y: Does the Hype Add Up?" *Sprout Social*, September 1, 2015. http://sproutsocial.com/insights/Gen Z-vs-gen-y/. Retrieved August 11, 2016.

12. Amy Bushatz, "Three Military Parent Tips for Generation Z," *Spouse Buzz*, July 20, 2016. http://www.spousebuzz.com/blog/2016/07/3-things-military-parents-should-know -about-generation-z.html. Retrieved August 24, 2016.

13. Barry and Murphy, *Flagging the Screenager*, 54.

14. Stacey Steinberg, "Five Truths about Parenting Generation Z," *Huffington Post*, May 13, 2016. http://www.huffingtonpost.com/stacey-steinberg/5-truths-about-parenting -generation-z_b_7249302.html. Retrieved August 24, 2016.

15. Yvonne Chee, "Parenting Generation Z," *The New Age Parents Online Magazine*, October/November 2012. http://thenewageparents.com/parenting-generation-z/. Retrieved August 24, 2016.

16. Chee, "Parenting Generation Z."

17. Bushatz, "Three Military Parent Tips for Generation Z."

18. Steinberg, "Five Truths about Parenting Generation Z."

19. Steinberg, "Five Truths about Parenting Generation Z."

20. Chee, "Parenting Generation Z."

21. Bushatz, "Three Military Parent Tips for Generation Z."

2
Helping Parents Understand Generational Differences

Millennials will start feeling old at an office party when nobody understands their tales of reminiscing over iPods and MySpace.[1]

GENERATIONS: CONTEXTS, CATEGORIZATIONS, CHARACTERISTICS

Why is it important how Gen Z parents signal and support the rise of this new generation? First, all young people seek to find their place in society. All Americans have at one time sought to contextualize their existence as unique. Second, categorizing generations by events and culture provides each new generation elbow room among previous generations. In this sense, Gen Z share much in common with other emerging generations of the past. Third, behaviors and practices that challenge status quo often become challenges to those of previous generations.

Learning to live with and work alongside each generation is necessary for assimilation into American culture and reassuring that, on some levels, the new generation has a place. Parents and teachers understand that both share significant roles in the success of Gen Z.

As with all generations and their sociohistorical designations, there exist only ranges of decades to which each generation is universally recognized. Generational titles are somewhat arbitrary in nature. However, to appease demographers, historians, and sociologists—as well as educators—categories are established as points of cultural and generational separation. These usually hinge on one or more historical events.

Americans seem to enjoy categorization, such as *favorite* athletic teams, *best* cities to live, or where the *ultimate* coffee is served. As parents, each desires that their children attend the best schools, have the best teachers, and play on the best athletic teams. Experts tie each upcoming group of young people to specific events that occurred within their lives and with clear changes in culture. New generations cannot be identified by previous generations.

One thing often overlooked by emerging generations is the impact a previous generation has in fashioning the changes that result in diversion from the norm. Each generation owes a certain level of gratitude toward its forebears. One cannot exist without the others previously establishing themselves.

Generation categorization is like an historical neighborhood, based on technological advancements, employment figures, worldwide happenings such as tragedies and wars, and other cultural and societal features and events. A generation of young people identifies its childhood with a unique major event, such as September 11, 2001 (9/11), the Cold War, or a series of political events. Using this rationale, Gen Z might well be associated with President Donald Trump and his election of 2016. If not, his victory could signal the emergence of a newer populist generation of children yet to come.

All things considered, the consensus is that categorizing generations is arbitrary. It makes for good reading, however, among those who both agree and disagree[2] as to the era that should define each. For example, as the reader will see, there is fluidity between Gen X and Gen Y. There is overlap between the silent generation and baby boomers, which implies a fuzzy middle of separation, usually based on age.

Based on recent trends, the people defined as millennials and Gen Z would be highly offended if there was not a special designation for them. The rise of smart technology and online innovations are hallmarks of both.[3] Which generations provided most of the technology with which subsequent generations identify? Hence the point is made about generational overlap and fluidity. That being said, youth has its benefits; because the younger replace the older in society and in the workplace, what the younger bring to both is worth noting. The bottom line is that Gen Z is an outgrowth of the millennial generation, as well as its own generation.

Elements That Define Generations

Howe and Strauss summarize generation distinctions according to three elements. The first element to consider is whether members of a particular group within society sense that they are part of that group. The sensing of identity and belonging begins with childhood and continues into adulthood. The second element is couched in two questions: Is the set of beliefs like or unlike previous generations? Are these distinct enough to hold the adherents to those beliefs for an extended length of time? If so, then the longer the beliefs are held, the greater the chance that members of a similar age group are part of a generation.

Third, there must be consideration whether there are particular events in history, movements, or contextual moorings to which generations can attach themselves.[4] If so, then the chance of a generational distinction is greater. These three elements, when taken together, encapsulate what is meant by the term "generation."

That being said, most sociologists agree that the baby boom generation probably is the best defined today, and it establishes comparative generational criteria to which others can compare. In other words, the majority of today's grandparents have set the standard for generational descriptions.

Columbia sociology professor Tom DiPrete explains why so much interest is generated around the young and the old: "I think the boundaries end up getting drawn to some extent by the media."[5] The baby boom generation "had specific characteristics"[6] that tied it to a period of time and well-defined events and historic landmarks.[7] The media tend to focus on the generation of those who occupy most of the journalistic chairs, as well as those newer to the profession seeking to make names for themselves. For example, many newsrooms are filled with millennials and newly graduated Gen Z reporters.

Transcendent Features

A study performed at the European University of Pecs, in Hungary, demonstrated that certain features transcend generations, regardless of the nation or continent. This is very sensible, especially among nations and people usually exposed to Western culture.[8] Accordingly, Torocsik, Szucs, and Kehl assert:

> Generations are interconnected by common experience, life and common values. The interconnectivity is loose but significant in its nature. It is loose because members of generations experience a lot of different facts and life decisions which cannot really be considered uniform. However, there is a significant trend of values and common experiences which can connect these decisions and lead to conclusions that are differences between generations, and similarities within generations provide a framework for the decisions of the members of generations.[9]

Nicknames Can Be Signs of Affection

Although the recent political climate warned against the assignment of nicknames, most names that pop up in journals are means of assigning personality and identity to a group that eventually will be studied. Sometimes these nicknames are scientific or alphabetic, and even connote a bit of wry humor and hearty affection. However, previous generations always make up and apply these names to the newer generations. For example, those determined to be products of the "me generation" are not the only generation of young people in American history to focus on themselves. So the "me generation" certainly are not the only selfish generation, to which its nickname implies.

Baby boomers began to shun their nickname as they grew into adulthood and began to emulate more of an "us" mentality, rather than be associated as babies of a generation preceding them. As a result, it is quite clear that generations focusing on themselves and their lives at least flirt with the possibility of earning their own tag.

The fact is that all younger people focus on the "me" while they are discovering the "me" they need to be. Apologies to Theodore Geisel! If baby boomers and Gen Xers took on the nickname the "me generation," then millennials easily can be called the "me me me generation,"[10] because they tended to focus on themselves much more than their forebears.

Economics and politics come into play in each emerging generation. Accusations of irresponsibility seem commonplace, as previous generations lose sight of their own youth. The passing of time covers many indiscretions. Existing older generations wonder if the newer ones will ever grow up and get things right. Forgotten over time is that each generation grows into seeing itself as the best generation ever.

In the past, Americans were more apt to join groups. This reality dates back to early eighteenth-century observations by Alexis de Tocqueville, captured in his writings about the United States at the time. According to de Tocqueville, there is something unique about Americans of the late eighteenth and early nineteenth centuries. That is, the culture of the day expected members of communities to develop "habits and encourage citizens to think independently,"[11] yet people banded together, even putting aside differences when necessary.

How does Gen Z fit with these things in mind? Gen Z is exploring itself and finding where it fits in American society. Most observers of culture already understand the high priority today's generation places on devices. People grow up and make their mark in American history. Gen Z, like the generations before them, will make its own impression on our nation's history.

THE BABY BOOM GENERATION
(BORN BETWEEN 1946 AND 1964)

The baby boom generation, or "baby boomers," as they are nicknamed, were born after World War II and encompass the beginning of the Cold War period with the Soviet Union. Boomers were preceded by the greatest generation—those who fought and died in World War II.[12] The boomers are also the children of what has also been nicknamed "the silent generation," due to their reputation for being "withdrawn, cautious, unimaginative, indifferent,"[13] as well as not necessarily given to sharing information about themselves and their families. Previous to the boomers and the silent generation (1925–1946) was the GI generation, described as born between 1901 and 1924. Presidents who served from the GI generation through the baby boom generation range from Teddy Roosevelt through the Kennedy-Johnson administrations.

The baby boom generation is made up of the children of World War II and Korean War veterans, and is characterized as very "work-centric."[14] They also are children born to Vietnam veterans, marking the beginning years of the Vietnam War era. The boomers are the first to be called the "me generation." But there is overlapping use of this term, as it is also applied to Gen X, the children of the boomers.[15]

GEN X
(BORN BETWEEN 1965 AND 1980)

Generation X is a term given to children born during the period 1965–1980. Gen Xers are called the "me generation" by some. They were born during the height of the Vietnam War, the tumultuous civil rights struggles of the 1960s, and party to the marvelous technological feats of the Apollo space program culminating with Americans walking on the moon and returning safely to earth.

This generation also saw the end of the Vietnam War, the post-hippie era, and the voting age decrease to eighteen. Also, there was the rise of Motown and what is now referred to as classic rock music. Gen Xers also were the first generation to experience a president resigning from office, in Richard Nixon (1974), due to the Watergate scandal and threat of impeachment. They also experienced the tail end of long gas lines and the Iran hostage crisis under President Jimmy Carter's administration.

By the early 90s, the so-called Generation X . . . refused to be intimidated into buying the latest styles of jeans or running shoes, opting instead for the ugliest clothes they could find at the local thrift shop. Grunge style, like grunge music, was a revolt against marketing itself. . . . This made Generation X ripe for harvest by mass consumer brands . . . of course teens eventually got wise to the anti-marketing marketing campaign.[16]

Gen Xers wrestled with becoming untangled from their parents' generation by establishing various forms of protest. Presidents who served during the emergence of Gen X range from Kennedy through Reagan.[17] Consensus among researchers is that Gen X remains more concerned about the economy and finances than other generations.[18]

GEN Y MILLENNIALS
(BORN BETWEEN 1981 AND 2005)

Generation Y is a term given to children born during the years 1981–1995 (or 2005). The ending date depends on which researcher is asked. Gen Y grew up "not having to do a lot of math in their heads, thanks to computers"[19]; as a group, they have been called "the biggest age-grouping in American history."[20] They are also referred to as the "last large birth grouping that will be easy to generalize about."[21] Millennials, generally, are technology oriented but not technology addicted. This distinction clearly separates them from Gen Z.

Although millennials sometimes are referred to as another of the "me generations," implying self-centered focus and drive, many social scientists and scholars are not so quick to pigeonhole this generation.[22] After all, Gen Y shares years of overlap with Gen X. That being said, social scientists predict that millennials soon will outnumber Gen Xers, probably within a decade or so. In reality, if numbers included subsequent immigration of those credited with the millennial classification, millennials would be "well on their way to becoming America's first 100-million-person generation."[23]

Millennials, as they overlap with Gen Z, can both be classified under the umbrella term "net geners." As such, it is sometimes difficult to tell millennials apart from their more recent counterparts. Both generations find success from the opportunities that "arise from . . . familiarity with technology [and] multi-tasking style. . . . Challenges, on the other hand, include the shallowness of their reading and TV viewing habits, a comparative lack of critical thinking skills, naïve views on intellectual property and the authenticity of information found on the Internet, as well as high expectations combined with low satisfaction levels."[24]

Joel Stein considers the overlap of the millennials and Gen Z and suggests a distinct splintering between the two groups. He posits, "There are already microgenerations within the millennial group, launching as often as new iPhones, depending on whether you learned to type before Facebook, Twitter, iPads, or Snapchat. Those rising microgenerations are all horrifying the ones right above them, who are their siblings. . . . They're already so comfortable in front of the camera that the average American 1-year-old has more images of himself than a 17th century French king."[25]

Whatever the case, those born during this era were born when the Middle East was in turmoil and Jimmy Carter was in the last year of his presidency. In science, the Space Shuttle program was in full swing. The disastrous explosion of the Space Shuttle Challenger was seen live in 1986. Ronald Reagan subsequently served two terms as president, ushering in the end of the Cold War era.[26] Another example of the difficulty in pigeonholing generations, some researchers label what is commonly referred to as the millennial generation—those born in the 1980s and 1990s—as "generation me."[27] Presidents who served during this Gen Y range from Reagan through George W. Bush.[28]

In closing, millennials are the children of the baby boom generation who, to some extent, have "inherited the consequences of boomer behavior, which includes high spending and low saving for such things as retirements and their kids' futures, such as college educations."[29] To say baby boomers are used to having it their way "is an understatement."[30] There can be little doubt where the Gen Xers and millennials picked up some of their practices.

Contrast between Millennials and Gen Z

The overlap between millennials and Gen Z extends beyond a range of assigned years into shared traits among the generations. The decade of the overlap in question is 1995–2005. Millennials are highly concerned about their children and demonstrate this concern in myriad ways. Like Gen Xers, millennials have earned the title of "helicopter parents." There is nothing new about parents taking active roles in nurturing children, but Gen Y seems to have perfected the practice of making decisions for their children.[31]

Millennials are all about editing photographs, making certain that each edited photo places them in the best light. They are more likely to "graze for news at various times of the day, rather than consume it at set periods,"[32] whereas Gen Z is more raw and immediate, and "embraces living in the right now."[33] Gen Z usually makes news of their own and does this through Snapchat, as they chronicle their days in video snippets, selected by interest and value to their viewers.

Millennials are not that reliant on their self-videos as self-promotions. As Gen Z matures, it is predicted they will begin to adopt some of the online behaviors of the millennials. They will begin downloading and using apps such as Honey, Rapportive, Boomerang, KeyMe, and Songkick, among others.[34]

One major difference between the generations preceding millennials and Gen Z: it appears that Gen Z is "turning their back on TV, email, and the fake world of celebrity."[35] Gen Z is focusing more on themselves, whereas "idealistic millennials embrace the sharing economy as many will continue to steer clear of owning a car or their own home."[36] A second difference is found in the conclusion reached by the Pew Research Center's Global Attitudes project:

> Pew Research studies show millennials are more likely than older Americans to participate in news by sharing links, contributing comments, and posting their own material. They are more likely than their elders to judge news operation—especially Web-based offerings—based on the willingness of a news organization to allow comments and contributions from users and to be transparent about its operations. Millennials are more likely to say search engines and social media steer them to local news and information on a variety of topics, including most dimensions of civic news such as local government, political news, and educational news.[37]

A third difference is that millennials are more likely to live with their parents, but not for the reasons many would assume. Another Pew Research study, released in the spring of 2016, reported that "for the first time in the modern era, living with parents edges out other living arrangements for 18-to-34-year olds."[38] This change is the first time in 130 years that such a cultural phenomenon has occurred in American society. Millennials may take up residence to assist financially, especially if hardships befall their parents. Between 14 and 17 percent of millennials "cited supporting parents as a current financial priority—double the rate of generation X workers."[39] Gen Z has not even begun to consider the future in these terms.

Something to Prove?

Millennials are discovering that they are undereducated, in terms of work and professional expectations of them, once they graduate from college. One millennial writes, "The biggest mistake I see twentysomethings make is thinking they have something to prove. You have nothing to prove. Nobody tells you this in college, or in high school, or middle school, or elementary school . . . we are all taught the opposite. We are taught we have everything to prove . . . we must prepare ourselves, or else nobody will want us."[40]

Couple this with the reality that more than one-third of millennials leave their jobs within one year of hire, and the essence of disenchantment and entitlement becomes more realistic.[41] The truth is that millennials have much less loyalty to their employers than they have toward themselves and their willingness to pursue self-interest.[42] Millennials had better take heed. One astute millennial writes, "It is only a matter of time before the Z Generation steps in."[43] There already is some bad blood between millennials and the upstart Gen Z.

Some are much more brutal in their assessment of millennials, which definitely spills over into Gen Z. The first truth that older generations seek to communicate to those in the millennial and Gen Z age ranges is this: "Nobody cares if you didn't have enough time. If your toilet flooded. If you weren't feeling well. If you're going through a rough time . . . in general, nobody cares. Everyone has stuff going on in their lives and it's on you to figure it out and stay on top of your responsibilities."[44] Your friends on Snapchat, Instagram, and Facebook might send you a like, or a heart icon, but the real world of business cares very little. For parents of Gen Z, this should serve as a wake-up call.

Millennials as Minimalists

Millennials are classified by researchers today as true minimalists. They are buying less of the things that tend to clutter one's life and spending more on experiences and events. This has serious implications for the economy and the marketplace. Some even wonder if for millennials the American dream is dead.[45] However, for millennials, "coffee shops have become the new office, collaboration has become the new competition, and mobility has become the new stability."[46]

Josh Becker, in his book *The More of Less*, explains that millennials are minimalists for a variety of reasons, not the least of which is seeing their parents' homes under water during the Great Recession in 2009, the student debt with which they graduated, and the fact that they graduated and entered "one of the worst working environments in modern history."[47] Millennials, unlike those in Gen Z, prefer financial stability to securing their dream jobs.[48]

Some 88 percent of millennials desire to live in an urban setting, and one-third of this generation is willing to pay more to do so. However, two-thirds of millennials prefer to live outside the urban areas, due to the complications and cluttered daily living, and exorbitant expenses for living quarters that sit vacant most hours of each day. Millennials also are delaying marriage and minimizing the immediate need to have families.[49] They would rather room together, as they did as coeds in college, than settle down. In fact, in so doing, by some accounts they are delaying adulthood.[50]

GEN Z
(BORN BETWEEN 1995 AND 2010)

Generation Z is a term given to children born between 1995 and 2010, which overlaps with millennials. Some extend the end period of Gen Z to 2015. However, inasmuch as Gen Z shares some traits with the millennial generation, some distinct differences also should be noted. Gen Z takes pride in the fact that certain characteristics of its generation are very unlike those of the millennials. First and foremost, members of Gen Z indicate they are likely to become frustrated more easily and much more quickly than previous generations.[51] This frustration sometimes is the result of being compared to millennials.

Gen Z was "born into a highly competitive global world."[52] In fact, the marketplace views Gen Z as "the most challenging, social but insecure group to enter the marketplace."[53] Some of this is the result of impatience due to information access and the notion that problems can be solved by looking up answers on Google or some other search engine on the Internet.[54] Descriptors assigned to Gen Z include *challenging* and *impatient*.

To some degree, all emerging generations can be described as challenging and impatient. However, Gen Z gets its impatience from somewhere and not by osmosis. Gen Z parents have stepped in to make certain their children do not miss the mark they established for them, in terms of family and future expectations. Consequently, children have not been allowed to experience the depths of failure and have been shielded from the real world. Their insecurities are based in emotion and collaborative groupthink. In fact, Gen Z thinks more highly of themselves, their potential contributions to the marketplace, than generations preceding them.[55] Their impatience is the result of several factors, not the least of which is Gen Z parental expectations, hyped by immediate access to each other through communication devices.

Gen Z's Hyper-Emotional Decision Making

Gen Z relies on emotions much more in decision making. Part of this emotional decision making is the result of the roles that Gen Z allows technology and the Internet to play in their daily lives. Another part of this emotional basis stems from their schooling, which emphasized learning by emotions and feelings. Rather than being asked, "What do you think?," Gen Z would rather be asked, "How do you feel?"

Today's young people are "hyperconnected. Always on."[56] Decisions often are being made while in a hyper-emotional state and are conditioned to respond accordingly. Specifically, Gen Z live at a time when "people are linked continuously through tech devices to other humans and to global intelligence."[57] Other generations also have this access. However, Gen Z—especially Z teens—has been "at the forefront of the rapid adoption of the mobile internet and the always-on lifestyle it has made possible."[58] This adoption has had an impact upon Gen Z. It is an environment that plays on emotions and is self-feeding, in that while online there is the availability of an entryway, if chosen, providing an always enabled elevated condition of emotions.

Gen Z in the Workplace

Gen Z understands their weaknesses in the marketplace going forward. As Ricoh-Europe CEO David Mills underscores, "Generation Z has high expectations from their employers—and so they should. Why shouldn't flexible and remote working truly become the norm? . . . But despite being demanding, Generation Z are also acutely aware of their workplace weaknesses, and believe they have a lot of skills to learn to be effective at work. In fact, self-critical Generation Z think they have more work to do to develop their skills than any other generation does. . . . Baby Boomers agree that Gen Z needs to develop in this area."[59]

As Gen Z continues to emerge and blend into the workforce, they will begin to replace retiring baby boomers and others. There is an economic reality to consider. "An unprecedented four distinct generations—baby boomers, Generation X, Generation Y and Generation Z—will be working side by side, each with their own styles, skill sets and worldviews. So how will they get along?"[60] This question will be answered in time.

Work together they must. Digital natives must be patient and learn to get along with the generations already resident in the workplace.[61] The same goes for those already employed for years, from each of the previous generations. Gen Z has its own unique perspectives and practices. Its members want to land their dream jobs, and chances are they have scoped out these jobs from the Internet.[62] But does Gen Z know what traits they must bring to the marketplace?

The Traits of Gen Z in the Marketplace

The traits Gen Z will bring to the marketplace include:

- a customization of the existing rules to shape these rules more to their liking, leading to a *what is best for me* attitude;
- the need for regular, scheduled, and ongoing training to become better at their jobs;

- a learning style that is based in technology and does not avoid the reality of the twenty-first century global marketplace;
- a preference to communicate with coworkers on an interpersonal, face-to-face level, but one that does not minimize the device-driven world;
- entrepreneurial spirits, when faced with problems, and understanding that the need for solutions is neither binary nor dichotomous, which means
- a need for immediate and long-term feedback, essential not only for problem solving, but also for validating the person in the process;
- a decision-making process that is highly conversational, leading to interpersonal persuasion and consensus by a team of colleagues;
- styles of leadership that include a strong push for teaching leaders how to lead, mentoring leadership, and training leaders; and
- the expectation of change from the way things were done before they were hired.

These changes are expected to happen sooner, rather than later, or Gen Z workers say they will find greener pastures and employers who are more willing to acquiesce to their expectations.[63]

Some Gen Z college students feel they are entitled to set the rules in the workplace. One group of young college interns found out that policies are not a collaborative effort among workers seeking to make changes. The recent headline "Spoiled College Grad Demands New Dress Code at Job, Gets the Boot"[64] says it all. Gen Z's patience and flexibility will be challenges, to be sure. Time will tell if the generation will adjust.

The presidents who have served in office with the emergence of Gen Z include Bill Clinton, George W. Bush, Barack Obama, and Donald Trump.[65]

GENERATIONAL DIFFERENCES

Americans acknowledge that real generational differences exist between each generation. Gen Z is no exception. Sometimes conflict arises due to differences in the ways generations handle issues. Anyone who has spent time teaching in schools comes to understand this very early in their career. In terms of education, with Gen Z teachers should be flexible sometimes, yet firm at others. Parents and teachers must understand that their smart technology will be both a distraction and a disruption at home and at school. These distractions and disruptions, and ways to minimize and use them, are addressed at length in chapter 3 of the second book in this series in a section titled "Engaging Gen Z Students."[66]

Honorary Gen Z Membership

Generational differences sometimes present natural barriers, and these natural barriers need to be recognized and respected.[67] Being modern has its difficulties, as each generation has discovered. Being modern in a postmodern age is a lot like finding truth in a post-truth era. The fact is that names are assigned, but the practices sometimes do not reflect the monikers. The good news for moniker iconoclasts is that any generation can be an honorary Gen Z member.

Jacob Morgan of *Inc.* states, "Any employee . . . can fall into the Gen Z category, no matter if they are 22 or 52. . . . Gen Z is the group that takes it to the next level by using technology, hyper-connectivity, and collaboration to drive innovation and change."[68] These can be accomplished, regardless of the age group.

When it comes to fashion and attire, each generation has had its bouts and experiments with style, trend, and cultural statements. Gen Z is no different. In fact, the style for Gen Z is difficult to pin down. They mix and match their clothing while making every effort to come across as stylish, yet uncaring of what they wear. Basically, their style is not to have a style.[69] This nonstyle has a name.

The style that described Gen Z is called "NormCore . . . a unisex fashion trend . . . A fusion of the words 'normal' and 'hardcore.' NormCore fashion involved piecing together unpretentious, average-looking outfits that are often oversized and seemingly mismatched."[70] Teenagers often wear pajama pants and a shirt or blouse that do not fit together in color or pattern. This trend seemed to have taken hold first at college. A trend that began with unkempt, late students rushing to class now has reached elementary school.

Gen Z Breaks Free

Gen Z have many opinions about themselves. Like all generations before them, the desire to be free from the previous generation is not small. Areas where Gen Z claims exclusivity from the millennials[71] include:

- Gen Z practices selectivity instead of excessiveness in purchase and lifestyle (especially online).
- Gen Z would rather focus on what it can create, rather than working for others to curate.
- Gen Z sends photos, videos, and other images to friends and family, instead of relying only on texting. They are visual and emotive in their communications.
- Gen Z cares about issues and becomes involved with them emotionally. They are a generation of emotional doers, over and against those who are cognitive observers.
- Due to the abundance of celebrities, Gen Z tends more toward those celebrities who would influence them toward action and belief in purpose larger than fame and notoriety.
- Gen Z is more impressed with substance over style, which is why they tend to visit YouTube more than any other social media site.

Table 2.1. Comparison of Five American Generations

Category	Gen Z	Gen Y Millennials	Gen X	Baby Boomers	Traditionalists
Estimated Range of Birth Years Assigned	1995–2010+ Shares Broad Estimate Years	Broad 1981–2005 <u>Narrow</u> 1981–1994	1965–1980	1946–1964	1925–1945
Nicknames	Entitled Generation; Net Geners; iGen	"Me, Me, Me" Generation	Me Generation	Me Generation	Silent Generation; Traditional Generation; Greatest Generation
Presidential Administrations	Clinton; Bush 43; Obama; Trump	Reagan; Bush 41; Clinton; Bush 43	Johnson; Nixon; Ford; Carter	Truman; Eisenhower; Kennedy; Johnson	Coolidge; Hoover; FDR; Truman
Key Value Characteristics	Personal Entitlement; Work by Choice; Environmental Concerns	Realistic Personal Safety; Digital and Cyber Literacy	Skepticism Lack of Trust in Institutions; Adaptive to Technology; Self-Reliant	Optimism Questioning of Authority and Institutions; Skeptical	Loyalty Faith; Work; Not Wasting Anything
Historical Events That Influenced	Similar to Millennials; Digital Natives; Diversity; Marriage Redefinition; Progressive Politics; Social Paradigm Changes	Explosion in Tech Growth; Digital Natives; Progressive Politics; Diversity; Crimes and Gangs; Political Correctness	Television; Handheld Games; Personal Computer; Divorce Rate	Suburban Life; Television; Vietnam; Rock and Roll; Drug Culture	WWI; Roaring 20s; Great Depression; WWII; Korean War
Values	Similar to Millennials; Socially Conscious; Socially Active	Safety; Digital Literacy; Global Concerns	Self-Reliance; Technology	Idealism; Challenge; Competitive	Logic; Legacy; Common Sense

Goals in Life	Find Purpose; Work Smarter; Financial Success	Building Several Careers	Building Careers That Are Portable	Building a Career	Leaving a Legacy
View of Institutions	Work for Companies; Work Independently	Each Person Judged by His Works	Doubt of Institutions	Work for Change	Pledge Loyalty
Career Path	Several Paths to Success; Entrepreneur-ship	Several Paths to Success	Changing Jobs Is Necessary	Stay at One Job and Build	Stay at One Job
Technology	Radio; Telephone; Television; Personal Computer; Internet; Digital Smart Devices; Wi-Fi	Radio; Telephone; Television; Personal Computer; Internet; Digital Smart Devices; Wi-Fi	Radio; Telephone; Television; Personal Computer; Internet	Radio; Telephone; Television; Computer	Radio; Telephone; Television
Highest Levels of Education	College; Graduate School; Trades; Technology; Entrepreneurs	College; Graduate School; Trades; Technology	College; Graduate School; Trades	High School; College; Trades	High School; Trades
Incentives	Setting of Schedule; Work at Will; Entrepreneurship	Meaningful Work; PurposefulWork	Work to Attain Desired Lifestyle	Recognition; Title; Money	Intrinsic Motivation; Personal Satisfaction
Preferred Available Mode of Communication	Social Media; Smartphone Videos; Twitter; Instagram; Snapchat; Texting	E-mail, Texting; Social Media; Cell Phone; File Sharing; E-mail	Face-to-Face; Telephone; Cell Phone; E-mail; Instant Messaging	Face-to-Face; Telephone	Face-to-Face; Telephone

LIGHTHEARTED GENERATIONAL ANALOGIES FOR GEN Z PARENTS

Finding analogous comparisons for each of five generations can be fun even as it is challenging. Associating groups with sports teams or famous actors pays dividends for teachers seeking methods to break down difficult concepts. It also helps to ease some parental frustration, regardless of the generation. The same is equally true when attempting to draw conclusions by making assertions about generations. Breaking things down into more understandable concepts is what many teachers do best.

Students adore stories, regardless of the grade level. Stories and comparisons are used in classrooms all over the nation on any given day. More likely than not, some of the teachers' stories are embellished to make a larger point for students. Parents understand this modus operandi, as they relate what grandparents and their own parents shared with them.

Part of the experience of a classroom teacher is to have fun with differences and generalizations, while providing an understanding between points of distinction. This is the intent at this juncture. Because everyone enjoys some food items, the following analogies will serve two purposes: (1) to illustrate the differences that exist in the types of approaches to be taken toward generations and (2) probably increase the reader's appetite.

The Rations Generation

Lighthearted examples of generational differences can be explained in many ways. For this section, the differences will be illustrated in terms of food items. The *war generation*, or the World War II generation—and slightly before—can be referred to the "rations generation." Typically, this generation consisted of people who came from Europe with nothing in their pockets, yet, over time, made lives for themselves in the United States. Ellis Island usually is the location people associate with this generation's migration. The war generation suffered through the Great Depression of the early twentieth century, yet went off to fight in World War II.

Nothing could deter the ultimate success of the war generation, and they built this nation postwar, from the ground up, and brought the nation into a new era. This generation is also referred to the "silent generation," made up of "leftover rations." They did not sit around griping or whining. They were hard at work with their tasks and understood the sacrifices required to raise a family.

As with the difficulty of opening the cans of war rations, the war generation also was seen by some as uncompromising, and as firm on their exterior. They were also highly private in their finances and personal lives, rarely ever threw things away, and meted out discipline to children as necessary. Children spoke when spoken to, and were to be seen and not heard. The parents were the center of the family universe. The "rations generation" were known to be less emotional and much more purpose driven.

The Crusty-Bread Generation

The children of the silent generation, or war rations generation, are called baby boomers. This generation can be referred to as the "crusty-bread" generation. Like their parents, they are hard and firm on the outside but not difficult to open up. However, unlike their parents, baby boomers, when open, are much softer and airy on the inside. Adopting some of their parents' characteristics, this generation benefited from the hard work of their parents and were often told, *I want you to have it easier and better than we had it.*

Raising a family, becoming educated, and establishing a career were mainstays of the boomers. Because they were a bit more open and loving, baby boomers began to soften with the changes that resulted in economic prosperity, realizing the American dream of home ownership and stable jobs. Essentially, life became easier than it was for their parents.

The Pastry Generation

The children of baby boomers, Gen Xers, were privileged to accumulate so many material benefits that a bit of displacement occurred. Material goods were now competitors in homes. The children of baby boomers can be referred to as the "pastry generation." Generally, life was sweet for Gen X children. Boomers brought many technological advances to the American experience, and American youth had its fill of this sugarcoated sweetness. Consider what Bill Gates and Steve Jobs brought to the world of communications, computing, and technology. Families found larger homes, collected more material goods, and provided children with all sorts of games, technology, and many new ways to be entertained.

The Fila-Dough Generation

Gen Y millennials can be referred to as the "fila-dough folks." Millennials can be somewhat flaky but look good in the process. The sense of entitlement that pervades millennials results in their being puffed up and full of hot air at times. The humor that is found in this analogy of millennials is that they are stereotyped as camping out in their parents' basement until age thirty. One has to wonder how many parents of millennials have realized this stereotype.

The Cream-Puff Generation

Then there are those in Gen Z, who are referred to the "cream puffs," "the cup-cake kids," "snowflakes," and the "softies." Sweetness and frosting cover their soft and fluffy exteriors. When their psyches and hearts are opened, they ooze emotion and compassion. Hence, they are just as soft and puffed up about their demeanor as they are about what fills their lives on a daily basis.

Right and wrong for Gen Z are generally determined by feelings, not morality and truth, or even facts. Gen Z are as confectionary as they come. Through and through, they admire the feelings of love and proclaim that feelings of love are the main reasons for any relationship between humans.

Saving every animal's life and protecting the environment and every person from judgment are the main drivers for Gen Z. They try to accomplish this under the guise of tolerance. However, they practice intolerance of disagreement, which makes them feel bad. The cream-puff generation is viewed as far too soft and squishy. One has to be extra careful when handling them. When treated a bit too roughly, the sugar falls off, and they tend to fall to pieces.

Those at college who cannot stand to be around disagreement feel threatened by being challenged. They refer to these challenges as bullying and are quick to demand a zone of safety from any challenges to their identities, feeling, or thoughts. Such experiences cause them to head to their collegial safe places. There is no better place for cream puffs to be protected than a bakery.

One University of California at Berkeley student group, approximately one hundred students, recently proclaimed that they felt jilted because of their safe space location. So, the group decided to protest for a new location by blocking the university main entrance, the "Sather Gate for several hours . . . as part of their latest protest to be relocated to different club space on campus."[72] They blocked access to campus, invading the open space of all students in order to protest their own space. Hence, we have the cream-puff kids and their actions. Is this what parents of Gen Z children anticipated when they sent their children off to university and college?

CONCLUSION

Helping parents to understand their children is a weighty task. Experts abound with studies in hand to prove one point or another. These are all well and good. Yet, those who know their children best, the parents, are often locked in battles. Teachers often can assist in viewing these battles objectively.

Aside from parents and families, teachers spend the next largest amount of time with children. Gen Z children spend significant parts of their days at school and involved with extracurricular activities. Gen Z children can be extremely busy, both at school and at home. This is where technology enters the picture.

Gen Z has adopted technology as it would a member of its own family. Parents must understand this and learn to moderate both their children's usage of this technology and the need for it in their lives. Gen Z is a wonderful addition to American culture. Their ease and acceptance of technology are refreshing for previous generations. However, their addiction to this technology is not so much appreciated, except for the marketplace, which thrives on sales to the addicted.

Compassion, deep feelings over issues, and a spirit of entrepreneurship pervade this generation. However, Gen Z is not as gritty and resolute in the face of extreme adversity. Part of this is due to Gen Z parents' stepping in to bail them out. One only wonders what type of parent the now twentysomethings of the oldest of Gen Z will become.

In closing, Gen Z brings to the table a sense of entitlement. This entitlement mentality has resulted in expectations that are sometimes unrealistic and moving toward critical mass. The expectations placed on schools and colleges as protectors, stepping in so no harm is done to one's political, social, or demographic psyches, demonstrates how fragile Gen Z can be.

NOTES

1. Daniel Burros, "Gen Z Will Change Your World Again," *Huffington Post*, February 3, 2016. http://www.huffingtonpost.com/daniel-burrus/Gen Z-will-change-your -wo_b_9150214.html. Retrieved July 21, 2016.

2. Diana Obringer, "Boomers, Gen Xers and Millennials: Understanding the 'New Student,'" *Educause Review* 38(4): 37–47.

3. Aubre Andrus, "Gen Z vs. Gen Y: Does the Hype Add Up?" *Sprout Social*, September 1, 2015. http://sproutsocial.com/insights/Gen Z-vs-gen-y/. Retrieved August 11, 2016.

4. Sarah Keeling, "Advising the Millennial Generation," *NACADA Journal* 23 (Spring and Fall 2003): 30. Cf. Neil Howe and William Strauss, *Millennials Rising: The Next Great Generation* (New York: Vantage Books, 2000), 3–5 and 42–43.

5. Philip Bump, "Here Is When Each Generation Begins and Ends, According to the Facts," *The Atlantic*, March 25, 2014. http://www.theatlantic.com/national/archive/2014/03/here-is-when-each-generation-begins-and-ends-according-to-facts/359589/. Retrieved June 28, 2016.

6. Bump, "Here Is When Each Generation Begins and Ends."

7. Bump, "Here Is When Each Generation Begins and Ends."

8. Maria Torocsik, Kristin Szucs, and Daniel Kehl, "How Generations Think: Research on Generation Z," *Acta Universitatis Sapientiae, Communicatio* 1(23) (2014).

9. Torocsik, Szucs, and Kehl, "How Generations Think."

10. Joel Stein, "Millennials: The Me Me Me Generation," *Time*, May 20, 2013. http://time.com/247/millennials-the-me-me-me-generation/. Retrieved November 2, 2016.

11. Alexis de Tocqueville, *Democracy in America* (New York: Harper Perennial Modern Classics, 2006), 97, 113, and 213.

12. Tocqueville, *Democracy in America*, 97, 113, and 213.

13. William Strauss and Neil Howe, *Generations: The History of America's Future, 1584 to 2069* (New York: William Morrow, 1991), 279–85.

14. Dan Schawbel, *Promote Yourself* (New York: St. Martin's Griffin, 2013), 175.

15. Keeling, "Advising the Millennial Generation."

16. Douglas Rushkoff, *ScreenAgers: Lesson in Chaos from Digital Kids* (Cresskill, NJ: Hampton Press, 2006), 202–3.

17. Keeling, "Advising the Millennial Generation," 30.

18. Schawbel, *Promote Yourself*, 174.

19. Stein, "Millennials: The Me Me Me Generation."

20. Stein, "Millennials: The Me Me Me Generation."

21. Stein, "Millennials: The Me Me Me Generation."

22. Jean M. Twenge, *Generation Me: Why Today's Young Americans Are More Confident, Assertive, Entitled—And More Miserable Than Before* (New York: Simon & Schuster, 2014 [2006]), xi–xiii. Cf. Stein, "Millennials: The Me Me Me Generation."

23. Neil Howe and William Strauss, *Millennials Rising: The Next Great Generation* (New York: Vantage Books, 2000), 15.

24. Joel Hartman, Patsy Moskal, and Chuck Dziuban, "Educating the Net Generation: Preparing The Academy of Today for the Learner of Tomorrow," *Educause*, 2016. http:// www.educause.edu/research-and-publications/books/educating-net-generation/preparing-academy-today-learner-tomorrow. Retrieved July 21, 2016.

25. Stein, "Millennials: The Me Me Me Generation."

26. "Challenger Disaster," *History Channel Archives*, 2000. http://www.history.com/topics/challenger-disaster. Retrieved November 25, 2016.

27. Twenge, *Generation Me*, xi–xiii.

28. Keeling, "Advising the Millennial Generation," 30–31.

29. Steven Van Metre, "The Millennial Generation Deserves Praise, Not Criticism," *Bakersfield Californian*, July 11, 2016, 11.

30. Staff. "The 13 Apps We Millennials Use the Most." *Social Media Week*. December 13, 2014. Retrieved January 27, 2017. https://socialmediaweek.org/blog/2014/12/13-apps -millennials-use/.

31. Schwabel, *Promote Yourself*, 172–74.

32. Paul Taylor, *The Next America: Boomers, Millennials, and the Looming Generation Showdown* (New York: Public Affairs/Pew Research Center, 2015), 188.

33. Daniel Burrus, "Gen Z Will Change Your World Again," *Huffington Post*, February 3, 2016. http://www.huffingtonpost.com/daniel-burrus/Gen Z-will-change-your -wo_b_9150214.html. Retrieved July 21, 2016.

34. Henderson, "Five Genius Apps Millennials Use That You Don't."

35. Burrus, "Gen Z Will Change Your World Again."

36. Burrus, "Gen Z Will Change Your World Again."

37. "World Publics Welcome Global Trade—But Not Immigration," *Pew Research Center's Global Attitudes Project*, October 4, 2007. http://www.pewglobal.org/2007/10/04/ world-publics-welcome-global-trade-but-not-immigration/. Retrieved July 24, 2016. Cf. Pippa Norris and Ronald Inglehart, *Sacred and Secular: Religion and Politics Worldwide* (Cambridge, UK: Cambridge University Press, 2004), 189. Cf. also Taylor, *The Next America: Boomers, Millennials, and the Looming Generation Showdown*, 189.

38. Richard Fry, "For First Time in Modern Era, Living with Parents Edges Out Other Living Arrangements for 18-to-34-Year-Olds," *Pew Research Center*, May 24, 2016. http://www.pewsocialtrends.org/2016/05/24/for-first-time-in-modern-era-living-with-par ents-edges-out-other-living-arrangements-for-18-to-34-year-olds/. Retrieved November 21, 2016.

39. Kelli B. Grant, "More Millennials Are Giving Back to 'Bank of Mom and Dad,'" *CNBC*, August 24, 2016. http://www.cnbc.com/2016/08/24/turnabout-more-millennials-helping-mom-and-dad.html. Retrieved August 25, 2016.

40. Nicholas Cole, "The One Thing I Wish Someone Had Told Me before Starting My First Job (Written by a Millennial)," *Inc.*, July 25, 2016. http://www.inc.com/nicolas -cole/the-1-thing-i-wish-someone-had-told-me-before-starting-my-first-job-written-by-a .html. Retrieved July 26, 2016. Cf. Tyler Durden, "Seven Harsh Realities of Life Mil-

lennials Need to Understand," *Zero Hedge*, March 10, 2016. http://www.zerohedge.com/news/2016-03-10/7-harsh-realities-life-millennials-need-understand. Retrieved November 13, 2016.

41. J. T. O'Donnell, "The Real Reason 30% of Millennials Want to Ditch Their Employer within a Year," *Inc.*, August 3, 2016. http://www.inc.com/jt-odonnell/real-reason-30-of-millennials-want-to-ditch-their-employer-within-a-year.html. Retrieved August 3, 2016.

42. O'Donnell, "The Real Reason 30% of Millennials Want to Ditch Their Employer Within a Year."

43. Tamara Baker, "Skipping School Means Missing Out on Big Future Earnings," *Bakersfield Californian*, August 16, 2016. http://www.bakersfield.com/news/opinion/2016/08/15/community-voice-skipping-school-means-missing-out-on-big-future-earnings.html. Retrieved August 16, 2016.

44. Nicholas Cole, "Twenty Brutal Truths All 20-Somethings Need to Hear," *Inc.*, August 2, 2016. http://www.inc.com/nicolas-cole/20-brutal-truths-all-twentysomethings-need-to-hear.html. Retrieved August 3, 2016.

45. Nathan Bomey, "For Millennials, Is the American Dream Dead?," *Bakersfield Californian-USA Today*, December 10, 2016, B1.

46. Josh Becker, *The More of Less: Finding the Life You Want under Everything You Own* (Colorado Springs, CO: Waterbrook Press, 2016). Cf. Josh Becker, "Why Millennials Are Turning Toward Minimalism," *Becoming Minimalist LLC*, February 18, 2016. http://www.becomingminimalist.com/millennials/. Retrieved August 15, 2016.

47. Becker, *The More of Less* and "Why Millennials Are Turning Toward Minimalism."

48. Nina Zipkin, "Here's What the Future of Work Looks Like to Millennials and Generation Z," *Entrepreneur*, June 8, 2015. https://www.entrepreneur.com/article/247115. Retrieved November 3, 2016. Cf. Charisse Jones and Eli Blumenthal, "Millennials Seek More from Holiday Shopping," *Bakersfield California-USA Today*, December 9, 2016, 30.

49. Becker, *The More of Less*.

50. Becker, *The More of Less*.

51. "Generation Z Is the Most Challenging, Social but Insecure Group to Enter the Workplace," *Ricoh-Europe*, October 5, 2015. http://www.ricoh-europe.com/about-ricoh/news/2015/generation-z-is-the-most-challenging.aspx. Retrieved June 26, 2016.

52. Schawbel, *Promote Yourself*, 175.

53. "Generation Z Is the Most Challenging, Social but Insecure Group to Enter the Workplace."

54. Marty Nemko, "Generation Z: What You Should Know about the Generation That Will Soon Run Our World," *Psychology Today*, October 25, 2015. https://www.psychologytoday.com/blog/how-do-life/201510/generation-z. Retrieved July 21, 2016.

55. "Generation Z Is the Most Challenging, Social but Insecure Group to Enter the Workplace."

56. Janna Anderson, "Main Findings. Teens, Technology, and Human Potential in 2020," Pew Research Center, February 29, 2012. http://www.pewinternet.org/2012/02/29/main-findings-teens-technology-and-human-potential-in-2020/. Retrieved November 10, 2016.

57. Anderson, "Main Findings. Teens, Technology, and Human Potential in 2020."

58. Anderson, "Main Findings. Teens, Technology, and Human Potential in 2020."

59. "Generation Z Is the Most Challenging, Social but Insecure Group to Enter the Workplace."

60. "Get Ready for Generation Z," *Robert Half International, Inc., Enactus*, 2015. https://www.roberthalf.com/sites/default/files/Media_Root/images/rhpdfs/rh_0715_wp_genz_nam_eng_sec.pdf. Retrieved June 27, 2016.

61. Diane Smith and Monica Nagy, "Meet the Class of 2018: Digitally Fluent Gen Z," *Star-Telegram*, September 1, 2014. http://www.star-telegram.com/news/local/education/article3871560.html. Retrieved June 14, 2016.

62. Zipkin, "Here's What the Future of Work Looks Like to Millennials and Generation Z."

63. "Get Ready for Generation Z."

64. Tom Knighton, "Spoiled College Grad Demands New Dress Code at Job, Gets the Boot," *PJ Media*, June 29, 2016. https://pjmedia.com/trending/2016/06/29/spoiled-college-grad-demands-new-dress-code-at-job-gets-the-boot/. Retrieved June 30, 2016.

65. Torocsik, Szucs, and Kehl, "How Generations Think," 29–30.

66. Ernest J. Zarra III, *The Entitled Generation: Helping Teachers Teach and Reach the Minds and Hearts of Generation Z* (Lanham, MD: Rowman & Littlefield, 2017).

67. Ernest J. Zarra III, *Teacher-Student Relationships: Crossing into the Emotional, Physical, and Sexual Realms* (Lanham, MD: Rowman & Littlefield, 2013). See chapter 1, passim.

68. Jacob Morgan, "Generation Z and the Six Forces Shaping the Future of Business," *Inc.*, July 5, 2016. http://www.inc.com/jacob-morgan/generation-z-and-the-6-forces-shaping-the-future-of-business.html. Retrieved July 21, 2016.

69. "Meet Generation Z: #Normcore," *Sinews*, 2016. http://www.cbsnews.com/pictures/meet-generation-z/10/. Retrieved August 11, 2016.

70. "Meet Generation Z: #Normcore."

71. Andrus, "Gen Z vs. Gen Y: Does the Hype Add Up?"

72. Alexander Barreiro and Jessica Lynn, "Student Groups Block Sather Gate in Latest Protest for Relocation," *Daily Californian*, October 23, 2016. http://www.dailycal.org/2016/10/23/student-groups-block-sather-gate-latest-protest-relocation/. Retrieved November 2, 2016.

3

What Makes Gen Z Tick and
What Makes Them Ticked?

Our teenagers and young adults are so immersed in the world of technology that many of them are struggling to separate their online worlds from real life. To ignore the impacts of technology and social media on how our adolescents are developing would be very foolish.[1]

Whoever came up with the term Generation Z must know something the rest of us don't. Some have joked that the use of the letter "Z" might imply that Gen Z is the last generation before the end of the world as we know it.[2] The truth: Gen Z lives in a very different world than the world of their parents and grandparents.

Certainly, Gen Z faces many of the same struggles previous generations have faced. This may be especially true during those challenging and sometimes pesky adolescent through young adult years. Many Americans have heard recent stories about children still living in their parents' home at age thirty. The stereotype is that these "lazy moochers" remain unemployed and continue their daily existence by playing video games online. As mentioned in chapter 2, the same stereotype has been applied to millennials, in their supposed "selfishness," which makes sense because the two generations overlap somewhat. But as stereotypes go, only traces of evidence support them. Therefore, Gen Z is not alone in being marginalized.

Mapping various generations, depending on the undertaking and points of origin, is "not an exact science . . . the edges are squishy and the dates are squishy . . . [and] people often resemble their times more than their parents."[3] Often brushed aside, because of the similarities of issues faced by multiple generations, is just how the transcendent issues are interpreted and applied, particularly in an age of massive technological advancements, as the nation finds itself in the twenty-first century.

For example, the challenge of drugs was prevalent for baby boomers in the 1970s. From designer drugs to synthetics to opioids, Gen Xers and millennials also faced their own drug challenges. The sad fact is that they still do. The access to drugs, people making and selling them, is so much easier for Gen Z. State govern-ments that allow the legalization of some drugs for recreation exemplify the accep-tance and modification of generational differences of some federally illegal drugs.

Social media enhances awareness; and cell phones, Snapchats, and mobs are used to support or to protest an issue in a flash. Immediate attention is granted anything and everything these days, which has led to very different concerns for the "immediate gratification generation": Gen Z.

WHAT MAKES GEN Z TICK?

Gen Z is a visual generation. There is no coincidence that "body shaming" is a Gen Z buzz phrase. Antibullying and positive self-esteem campaigns mark the current cultural landscape. Unlike the past, today's visual, record-everything penchant comes with the immediate explosive replication of a message that, in the past, was spread mostly by word of mouth. Past generations used terms that are off limits for today. What is odd about today's antibullying is a certain ganging up on those willing to retain previous generation's terminology. Apparently it is acceptable to confront bullying today, by mob bullying and character shaming. Gen Z is learning to use its devices to harm exponentially those who have harmed others. Essentially, gang bullying and gang shaming, to stop bullying and shaming by others, is the new aggressive paradigm that has emerged for Gen Z and millennial participants.

Image Is Everything

Body image and physical appearance are not the same to Gen Z students. Just ask any model, or anyone who has used software to make herself look younger, or distorted for fun. Cell phones have apps that can change one's complete ap-pearance, as well as touch up a face or body. One's physical appearance often may be quite different than the body image portrayed online. Age is no longer an issue. Everyone can be improved; all the evidence required to prove this point is on personal social media pages. Ever notice how few people make it a practice to post their worst photos?

In the past, a discussion of body image inevitably would result in how a person felt about herself, one's self-esteem, and so forth. The same is still true for Gen Z. However, with the ability to post photos instantly, many times only the best are chosen. The difference between today's body imaging and reality of physical appearance is best observed in the cable program *Catfish*. The social media im-age a person sees is not necessarily the real physical appearance. The Internet can shape another person's emotions, and body imaging can either attract or distract viewers. Sadly, an increasing number of Gen Z young adults are posting more and more provocative photos, leading this author to coin a phrase, "Phot-hoes."

Personal Identity

Gen Z is the first generation to experience a new top-down, politically driven, technologically heightened personal identity movement. This movement assumes some of the past categories of previous movements, but adds a twist. True, today's movement focuses on sex and gender, as did some movements in the past. However, today's sex and gender issues are now found in choices of expression, as these choices form one's identity. Men and women, boys and girls are encouraged, if not expected, to believe they are not male or female, boy or girl at birth, if they feel otherwise. Terms are mere constructs today, Gen Z is told, and there are more than two dozen such gender and sexual constructs from which to identify and ultimately to choose. In the past, Gen X bragged, *if it feels good, do it*. Gen Z has modified this to, *if you feel it, you're it*.

Previous generations, although somewhat tolerant, do not understand the social and moral dynamics that are taking place within Gen Z. Maybe time will bring acceptance, or at least understanding. Every generation has had to endure hardships from its predecessors. However, understandable across generations is basic economics. Near the top of the list for Gen Z and their parents is illustrated in a recent TD Ameritrade survey. "Both Gen Z and their parents listed jobs and unemployment first when asked to identify their biggest concerns about the economy."[4] Along with the guarded optimism of Gen Z and their future, not all have the same sense of this emerging generation of workers. Some wonder whether Gen Z is more of an American phenomenon, or whether the generation and its characteristics span the globe.

EMOTIONAL MATURITY AND COGNITIVE DEVELOPMENT

Neuroscientists and other brain researchers have come to the conclusion most parents and teachers have known for years: the brains of males and females have major differences when it comes to emotional and cognitive maturity.[5] Some physicians and professionals are very concerned over the high reliance of Generation Z on technology. They are worried that the overuse and extreme reliance on technology is changing brain connectivity and leading Gen Z down the path toward another form of attention deficit disorder: Digital Attention Deficit Disorder (DADD).[6]

The Brains of Gen Z Teenagers

Despite trending and faddish social movements in one direction or another, certain biological characteristics mark the brains of children, of which Gen Z parents should be aware. For example, a girl's brain has 15–20 percent more neural activity at any given time than a boy's brain. The fact is that the brains of girls and boys are biologically different, and the same holds true for adults. But different *does not* mean one brain is superior to another, or that one gender can or cannot learn a certain skill or content area.

Harry Barry and Edna Murphy write:

> The male brain is slightly bigger, with more neurons; women score with more connections among all the parts of the brain. Men focus on individual issues, women on the bigger picture. The bridge between the two hemispheres of the female brain has more connections. . . . This explains why many women are multitaskers, with the uncanny ability to carry out a number of jobs simultaneously. The hippocampus is larger in women and the amygdala or "stress box" is larger in men. The speech area in men is almost completely situated in the left hemisphere while, in women, it involves both. There are also more neurons in parts of the female brain associated with language processing and comprehension. So women are naturally more talkative than men. Women tend to verbalize (sic) difficulties openly—often to each other—whereas men often have these conversations within themselves.[7]

Differences in activity in male and female brains enable different parts of the female brain to work simultaneously in ways the male brain does not. Another major difference neuroscientists discovered between the male and female brain, particularly among teenagers, is that the male brain tends to compartmentalize its activity into fewer brain centers than the female brain.

Girls and women have a greater number of nerve fibers in their brains than boys and men. The pressure receptors on the skin, as well as pain receptors in the brain, are less sensitive in the male brain than the female brain. Females feel pain differently in their brains than males do. Males feel pain, but their bodies and brains feel less pain than females' bodies and brains.

Physically, male brains have more gray matter; female brains, more white matter. Gray matter is a neurotransmitter, which acts to localize context, compartmentalize knowledge and experience, and assist in keeping brain activity relegated to certain parts of the brain. Conversely, white matter networks brain activity to different parts of the brain, including emotional and empathy centers. Parents should understand that one-size-fits-all child rearing probably is not the best approach to employ. People are different, and teachers should be aware of this as they teach.

The male brain shuts off—or as neuroscientists state, *enters a rest state*—more times a day than the female brain tends to do. Is there little wonder why males are fully attentive one moment and suddenly fast asleep the next? The implications for parents and teachers are similar in terms of understanding these biological differences. Dr. Caroline Leaf clarifies: "Science shows us that the male brain moves into the rest state to rejuvenate more frequently than does his female counterpart. This does not mean he has switched his brain off ladies! His brain is rebooting in these rest states, and he does it differently to you. What's important to remember here is that when men move into their rest states to reboot, they are not trying to ignore you or be mean; he reboots through withdrawal! When a woman enters her rest state she is likely to be more talkative and extroverted because she reboots through communication and the famous (or infamous?) 'getting it all out.'"[8]

Brain Biology and Chemical Differences

The male brain, especially in the right hemisphere, has more neural centers than the female brain. This accounts for a difference between boys and girls in the ways they focus objects and move around in physical space. For example, researchers have found that males spend more time than females in manipulating and moving objects, such as balls and testing cubes. Researchers have given these objects and their manipulation the term "relational intermediaries." Relational intermediaries are objects that make relationships much more comfortable for males.

Females process information and life experiences in different parts of their brain than males—even when males and females' experiences occur at the same time. As a result of these differences in brain structure, energy levels for males and females are different. Although it is not politically correct to assert the following, male energy is channeled more toward hitting each other as a bonding mechanism and bantering that incorporates other dominance and aggressive activities through which males demonstrate love and affection. Parents probably see this at home when their sons constantly are touching other siblings.

The hippocampus, which is the major memory center in the brain, generally is less active in males than in females. The emotional moments that occur last much longer for females in their memories than in the memories of males. However, for the males, the moments are larger but lose their luster more rapidly.

Females' occipital, parietal, temporal, and frontal lobes generally are all more active than those areas in males' brains. Female brains generally have more linkages to senses (seeing, touching, tasting, etc.), feelings, and the word-making centers of the brains. Most adults are aware that females are much more verbal. Females, then, according to neuroscientists, often have greater sensorial experiences adjoining their surroundings at any given moment. Female brains store more of their memories, and these memories are hooked to the emotional centers of their brains.

In terms of chemicals, young males have between ten and twenty times more testosterone than young females. Testosterone is a risk-taking, aggression chemical. Males have less of the bonding chemical oxytocin. Males do bond with each other, but they tend not to reach out and bond with as many people as girls do. They often need more help in finding crucial bonding opportunities and moments. Parents should be the primary catalysts toward these moments.[9]

Males generally have less serotonin, a chemical that calms the brain's impulsivity, moving through the frontal lobes of their brains. The frontal lobe is the decision-making area of the brain. With less serotonin, males generally are more physically and socially impulsive; consequently, they have more trouble exercising their action filters. Conversely, females tend to be more consequential in their thought processes, especially during adolescent years. This means girls weigh consequences differently than boys.

In terms of addiction and the developing brain, the consensus among the medical community may best be understood in the following explanation: "If adolescents' brains are exposed to nicotine regularly, the resetting of their brain pleasure systems has been shown to make them more prone to developing addictions to other drugs and substances during their lifetimes."[10] Furthermore, because of the effects of substances on the developing brain, "particularly the dopamine system and on its connections between key regions, there is a string link between cannabis use and early psychosis. . . . There is also a lot of debate as to whether the usage of cannabis between the ages of twelve and nineteen triggers depression."[11]

As parents can attest, males and females are different in many ways. Some of these areas include: (1) different approaches to paying attention, (2) differences in the ways they think about and envision their futures, (3) unequal motivation toward completing tasks they are given to accomplish, (4) various methods to de-stress in the middle of taxing situations, (5) work differently toward others with whom they seek to relate, (6) vastly different periods of time within which they find themselves biologically and chemically bored in their brains and emotions, and (7) converse on different levels verbally and through body language.

WHAT MAKES GEN Z SO SPECIAL?

Each generation believes in its achievements and legacy. Generations of the past are proud to extol the virtues of innovation and the technologies invented. They are quick to point out America's victories and domination over world systems that threatened our way of life. Industrial and economic booms built the middle class in America. But what makes the emerging Gen Z so special? Is it because they believe they are, based on what they have been told? Are the answers found in the beliefs of the developing brains of this emergent generation? Michael Gazzaniga, former member of the President's Council on Bioethics, might agree. He writes, "Neuroscience teaches us . . . that the brain wants to believe. We are wired to form beliefs."[12]

The details of the formation are sketchy for a generation not yet fully wired in their beliefs and thinking. The addition of technology throughout this development may have deleterious effects upon what could be a "set of biological responses to moral dilemmas, a sort of ethics, built into our brains."[13] Beliefs are one thing. Actions and accomplishments are another. If this is accurate, then interrupting the normal and natural brain development could be hazardous for society, cause some interesting beliefs to develop in the minds of a generation, and affect maturation of frontal lobes.

What's in a Name?

To begin, Gen Z is not the same as the millennial generation. Gen Z "tend to be independent,"[14] and they are quite impatient about following prescribed patterns before achieving success. In a word, many Gen Z are highly entrepreneurial in their thinking; and thanks to social media, which has always been a part of their lives, Gen Z is more adept at engaging friends and acquaintances in a global sense.[15] This thinking carries over to their actions. Gen Z is "already out in the world, curious and driven, investigating how to obtain relevant professional experience before college."[16] However, it is Gen Z's belief system that drives its emergence.

Some of the names that have been applied to Gen Z beliefs and actions are quite interesting. They have been called the "next big retail disrupter,"[17] and a generation whose parents play "an equally powerful role in shaping their collective outlook."[18] As with all generations, sociologists and educators—even politicians—weigh in, attempting to garner the glory for labeling a generation. At least eight names have been attached to Gen Z: (1) iGen, (2) Post-Millennials, (3) Homelanders, (4) Digital Natives, (5) Selfie Generation, (6) Generation Zed, (7) Generation Firsts, and (8) Generation iCan.[19] Those studying Gen Z are piecing together this unique generation, and they are noticing that "the caution, the focus on sensible careers . . . Generation Z starts to look less like brash millennials and more like their grandparents (or in some cases like great-grandparents)."[20] Gen Z believes it is upstart and extra special, yet lacks the unique contributions that have marked past generations.

Some Generational Differences

One major difference between the previous generation, the millennials of Gen Y, and Gen Z appears to be the preference of the latter to seek in-person interactions with people, rather than strictly online.[21] To the glee of advocates of development of emotional intelligence, all indicators are that Gen Z is demonstrating a high level of willingness to develop proficiency and understanding of this intelligence. The blend of social interactions and emotional intelligence appears to align Gen Z with Robert Goleman and Marty Nemko's perspectives on emotional intelligence and social engagement.

In his book *Social Intelligence: Beyond IQ, Beyond Emotional Intelligence*, Goleman captures the essence of an underlying generational difference between Gens Y and Z. However, he cautions, "Simply lumping social intelligence within the emotional sort stunts fresh thinking about the human aptitude for relationship, ignoring what transpires as we interact. This myopia leaves the 'social' part out of intelligence."[22]

Gen Z students are closer to their parents than students were in previous generations. The reasons for the relationship closeness are twofold. First, more Gen Z students are homeschooled that any previous generation. This enables them to spend more time with their families in a learning environment. Second, Gen Z students are closer to their parents because their parents tend to watch the same television and cable programs. They spend time on the Internet together, play video games, and enjoy similar music styles.[23]

Another difference between the two generations is that "many Gen Zers intend to go to traditional college, but after that, their lives and careers are likely to be anything but traditional."[24] Gen Z students do not like to lose, and they feel deeply about everyone being treated the same. Ribbons, trophies, and allowances are expected. Gen Z believes strongly that *if someone else has it, we should have it too.*

This mind-set is observed in the playing of video games, where there is always a solution, always an ending and significant accomplishment. Gen Z think problems can be solved, games can be won, and most people can have what they desire, even without exerting the same level of energy to attain it. This is the way they are wired, and their devices reinforce easy access to answers to life's problems, and the social network reinforces many of their beliefs.[25]

MICRO-AGGRESSIONS

Any author who attempts to understand Gen Z must address the more recent phenomenon of micro-aggressions. Previous generations used to call these sarcasm, subtleties, snide one-liners, and teasing. Just a few years ago, a blurted comment usually would bring a common retort, or even a playful jab in the stomach. But things are vastly different today. Institutions are taking on the roles of parents to protect students from having their beliefs challenged or their feelings hurt.

The term micro-aggression might benefit from retooling. At the risk of offending the softer Gen Z student, professors might in jesting substitute a new term: "micro-regression," implying Gen Z is stunting its maturity by accepting a new cultural paradigm.

Some college campuses today provide evidence of a new version of protest. Groups are disallowing on-campus micro-aggressions by students toward others with whom they disagree. For example, bringing a controversial speaker onto a college campus might cause students such inner turmoil that they would be unable to take exams, or even attend classes. Ironically, they would, however, be able to sit at the coffee shop and share their despair with others, smoke marijuana, or join a macro-protest to demonstrate the impact of the assault on their beliefs or their hurt feelings.

Micro-aggressions may be based on emotions and psychological disturbances, but they also are plays on words for those who enjoy statistics. The question is who or what has ingrained in Gen Z that it is no longer all right to be offended? Imagine some of the small and persistent statements, or insinuations in books—or even comments from the past—that, if used today, may cause serious emotional upset.[26] As a side note, this is one very good reason why teachers, parents, and students of mixed generations should avoid being friends on social media sites. The chances of offending someone or some group, or having something misinterpreted rises with each level of generational proximity surpassed.[27]

Recently, Gen Z's propensity to be protected from what may challenge their intellect or emotions played out in the media. This "upset" over Bernie Sanders losing in the 2016 primaries, followed by Hillary Clinton's loss to Donald Trump in the general presidential election, caused emotional distress on many college campuses. Anyone supporting Donald Trump, by merely posting a campaign placard, was guilty of causing harmful micro-aggressions, leading some young women toward being "too overrun with emotion."[28] This was, in fact a reason given why some students would be unable to perform as they would expect on the assessments for high school and college.

Generation Z, for all of their wonderful additions to American society, are stereotyped as far too sensitive, far too easily offended, and expect the morals and ethics to change to be socially just for all. They think their beliefs should overtake the sensibilities of previous generations. This stereotype is being played out at college, as the reader will discover. Consider a few examples:[29]

- Yale University: Professor responds to heartfelt notes from students in shock over the election of Donald Trump as president and makes an exam optional.
- University of Northern Colorado: A student writes "free speech matters" on only one of 680 *#languagematters* posters, reminding all students to use politically correct language.
- DePaul University: A poster with the caption "Unborn Lives Matter" was viewed as bigotry.
- Bowdoin College: After a sombrero and tequila dress-up party, some students were provided counseling by the college due to cultural trauma the party caused.
- Oberlin College: Students proclaimed that their classwork was causing them undue stress and therefore resulting in physical and emotional breakdowns. The students could not balance their political activism and the work required for their classes. A faculty guide for supporting sexual assault victims instructed the faculty that anything could be a trigger, including phrase, smells, songs, persons, places, and so forth; this faculty guide has been removed.[30]
- California State University, Los Angeles: The university administration allowed a controversial speech to be presented but had to deal with its emotional fallout. Three months after the fact, the university established healing spaces for the distraught.

- Indiana University: Students on campus were in an uproar because a priest was on campus. Because he was wearing a white robe and a rope belt, and carrying rosary beads, he was accused of being in the Ku Klux Klan.

Furthermore, a UCLA professor recently caused a student sit-in protest, because of a perceived micro-aggression. It seems that some students did not like the way a professor's instructional methodologies were employed and generally how the class was run. As a result, a small group, led by one student, reported the professor through an official letter of complaint to the university.

The complaint centered on a preposterous issue: "In the course of correcting his students' grammar and spelling Rust had noted that a student wrongly capitalized the first letter of the word *indigenous*. Lowercasing the capital *I* was an insult to the student and her ideology."[31] Is it possible that we have arrived at the social-educational zenith, where a professor, teacher, or administrator is reprimanded merely for questioning the notion, or perception, of a student? Unfortunately, the answer is, "Yes."[32] Professors today must be wary of the smallest offenses sowing the seeds of discontent and upset.[33] Parents must ask themselves, "What have we done to our children that correcting them now amounts to an offense?" When our nation arrives at the point where iPhone users are offended at Samsung smartphone users, we will have reached our cultural nadir.

Are the students even aware that the accusation and drafting the letter of complaint are more aggressive than the professor's actions? Had they stopped to realize, they would have understood their actions as a macro-aggression toward someone seeking to cause them discomfort for their betterment as writers. This is a serious weakness among Gen Z. Using emotions to determine reality and what is important in life is something Gen Z parents must be aware of so they can work toward balance with their children.

The late British philosopher C. S. Lewis seems to have predicted what would happen on college campuses in his 1944 book *The Abolition of Man*. In it, Lewis warns "people about the corrosive effects of subjective morality. . . . He traces the principles of conscience, the reasoning behind calling something 'right' or 'wrong,' throughout different cultures and religions. . . . While many attack the 'traditional morality,' it is the building block for all moral values, and such principles as the Golden Rule."[34] Lewis has a point. Things seems to have shifted toward the elevation of *payback by one group toward another*.

The so-called underprivileged of the past are now empowered as privileged, seeking a "pound of flesh" to shut down anything they sense is untoward or secondarily overheard as even remotely offensive. Part of this entitlement attitude for some Gen Z students stems from universities and colleges willing to meet the demands of the few by acquiescing to intellectual safe spaces, emotional healing spaces, and new policies asking professors to include "written or spoken warnings . . . to alert students that course material might be too traumatic for people with particular life experiences."[35]

On some campuses, those on the extremely sensitive fringe are convinced they must give permission for anything close to an offense to occur, by requiring such "trigger warnings," and they are quick to label statements, comments, or something academically formal from a "privileged" group as a micro-aggression. These terms began to emerge on college campuses during the Obama administration and had their genesis in blogs on feminism and discussions in forums on sexual violence.[36] Macro-aggressive dissent is employed to shut down perceived micro-aggressive freedom of speech. In a democracy, and particularly at institutions of higher learning, both forms of speech should be allowed, without one side seeking to shut down the other.

MENTAL FILTERING

Mental or negative filtering is the action of selecting something negative, dwelling exclusively on it, and drawing conclusions based exclusively on the negative premises. For example, if a child does something troublesome in school, a teacher might identify the child by his or her action. Dwelling on the negative action of the child conditions the teacher's response to conclude other negatives about the child.

Another example is what transpires on secondary and postsecondary campuses, when students are demonized for belonging to one student, political, or social group. Such negative filtering in based on emotions, and students who practice this rarely use rational thought to see both sides of an issue. Consequently, this type of filtering seldom allows positive statements to be made about the group that has been deemed problematic. In fact, the mere attempt at reason or balance is seen as offensive, and an act of aggression toward the case initiated originally.[37] A good example of this is the Black Lives Matter protest; anyone who suggests "all lives matter" is labeled racist by adding something beyond the exclusive statement.

On college campuses we see a brand of subjective protectionism running wild. Haidt and Lukianoff describe this phenomenon as "vindictive protectiveness."[38] It "minimizes the value which traditional morality (and arguable conscience itself) places on the pursuit of truth. To nearly all scholars who have gone before, the pursuit of truth is worth being offended or having your feelings hurt. Students today seem to disagree. . . . Vindictive protectiveness is a warped morality. In the name of equality, campus culture elevates the importance of some groups over others, and silences dissenting opinions in favor of groups that are seen as underprivileged."[39] VP is accomplished by consciously labeling a group as "privileged." It also is responsible for the creation of safe places for students to be with each other without having their feelings hurt, and aggressively squashing dissent by marginalizing and name-calling. This labeling has filtered down to elementary schools. Are these the values associated with higher learning that Gen Z parents prefer their children to master?

THE SCARECROW AND THE TIN MAN

The classic movie *The Wizard of Oz* portrays a scarecrow as a being with no brain, and a tin man as a clunking, rusting metal creature with no heart. Their characters acted a certain way prior to obtaining their intelligence and emotions. Similarly, children are viewed in certain ways as their brains develop and their emotions temper. Once they fully mature, they discover they are very different from those years before maturity.

Expert opinions are all over the neurological landscape regarding efforts to standardize knowledge about the brains of Gen Z. The brains of the technologically wired generation process information somewhat differently than the brains of previous generations. In fact, the brains of Gen Z are wired so very differently that some believe they "function better with input from a variety of sources."[40] Gen Z really mean it when they say they can learn while listening to music or having what others would call distractions occupy the same attention space. What Gen Z mean and what is actual are quite different.

There are good reasons for this lack of congruency. The freshness of Gen Z leaves much to be considered, in terms of the impact on them and their impact on society as a whole. Once they go off to college, the more developed brains of Gen Z are being exposed to a much different form of learning.

There seems to be more emotion-centric development with the brains of Gen Z females. One reason is the method of emotion-based instruction that students experience in schools. Add to this their technology reliance, and students begin to associate their emotions to life around them a bit differently. Repetition of emotional expression via social media draws out one's automation to certain behaviors and practices. Even so, "In spite of this fact, parents, teachers, and health professionals attempt to reach young people on an intellectual level. The only effective mode of communication is one which evokes an emotional response."[41]

Barry and Murphy theorize, "When we are waking up, it is the emotional brain which comes to first, before the logical brain. This is why so many adults and adolescents notice symptoms of anxiety first thing in the morning—even before their logical brain has had a chance to review what is coming up that day."[42] Likewise, "mainly due to hormonal differences, there is a delay in the development of the male brain compared to the female brain, which is most obvious in early adolescence."[43]

As serendipity would have it, this chapter is being written in the midst of kitchen remodeling, with workers heavily engaged in conversations about their young adult children. The comments pertain to the challenges of raising males versus females, and the subsequent differences in their actions. One worker was quite boisterous in elaborating on the choices made by a nineteen-year-old who was "lazy, and not thinking clearly" about a new love of his life. Apparently the young man wanted to marry and leave college to focus on this new relationship, all without a plan to sustain it.

AN INCH DEEP AND A MILE WIDE

Is Gen Z deepening its knowledge and understanding of life by adding more sophisticated technologies? Are Gen Z children growing as healthy people in mind and body, or are they becoming more distant, hovering around the surface of life? A trend in American culture advertises the proposition that doing more things in life deepens identity. Conversely, great is the disagreement whether smart technology, as one of these things, has resulted in widespread cultural superficiality.

Patrick Deneen laments what he refers to as the generation of "know-nothings," because "they possess accidental knowledge, but otherwise are masters of systemic ignorance. It is not their 'fault' for pervasive ignorance of western and American history, civilization, politics, art and literature. They have learned exactly what we have asked of them."[44] The American educational system is not broken, according to Deneen. He contends that today's students are products of a system working full-force and achieving its goals. Deneen asserts, "What our educational system aims to produce is cultural amnesia, a wholesale lack of curiosity, history-less free agents, and educational goals composed of content-free processes and unexamined buzz-words like 'critical thinking,' 'diversity,' 'ways of knowing,' 'social justice,' and 'cultural competence.'"[45]

In short, the American educational system is producing more social activists who have less knowledge of the past. The result is acting on emotions, not so much on anything of cognitive substance. Children can search and find things on the Internet; that tends to make them think they are smarter. However, the fact that drivers drive well does not mean they understand automotive functioning or can repair a car.

This "pseudo sense of smartness" is precisely the result of the notion propagated by those with designs on a one-size-fits-all set of standards called Common Core. Making education more difficult does little to motivate the already unmotivated. Parents understand this well. If a child cannot accomplish one or two basic, required tasks around the home, it would be near insanity to foist on him a hefty to-do list.

American students have become the crowning achievement "of a systemic commitment to producing individuals without a past for whom the future is a foreign country, cultureless ciphers who can live anywhere and perform any kind of work without inquiring about its purposes or ends, perfected tools for an economic system that prizes 'flexibility.'"[46] Gen Z parents ought to be very concerned about this.

WHAT MAKES GEN Z TICKED?

The simple answer to the question posed in this section title is that *many times they have no idea why they are angry*. Each generation has its causes and passions—the likes of which sometimes appear irrational. When a discussion ensues about what angers or ticks off a generation, it is really honing in on causes and issues about which a particular generation feels strongly. For example, during World War II, people feared whether Japanese Americans would be loyal to the United States or to the nation of their heritage. The Greatest Generation, followed by the baby boomers, had a different perspective on the enemies faced in the 1930s and 1940s.

The boomers and Gen Xers wondered about the Cold War and communism. Protests began to emerge, and antiwar sentiments arose in the nation well into the 1970s. Government corruption was a major area of concern. Whether the issue is terrorism abroad, or homegrown lone wolf, self-radicalized terrorist groups, social justice, or the Black Lives Matter movement, Gen Z is right in the middle of them.

Australian social researcher Mark McCrindle senses that researchers are detecting a "move away from the past decade's rampant materialism, a stronger emphasis on social justice and a generation of highly educated, technologically savvy, innovative thinkers."[47] This is an excellent point to consider. Regardless of the nation or continent, it seems to have an overarching oneness with Gen Z. This oneness is made more prominent because of the Internet and the immediacy of communications.

Culture simply does not change by itself. Schools and colleges have enormous impacts on students. They directly shape and can sometimes spur advocacy for a cultural paradigm, using political correctness, social justice, and protest as the evidence. Public education has become a hotbed of social activism and experimentation, and Gen Z is in the middle of the experiment. As a result, Gen Z has been "branded as a welcome foil to the Millennials."[48]

In the midst of the experimentation, Gen Z students want to graduate and obtain jobs that extend the social justice aspects of their education, and plan to have sociocultural impacts in the workplace and in local communities.[49] Through technology and social media, as well as by those whom they respect, Gen Z is exposed to influences that parents can sometimes counteract.

For example, college faculty openings in education, sociology, or the humanities include a hidden agenda of disqualification, in terms of an applicant's view on things such as social justice and noncitizen enrollees. Such a protective political environment at college does little to expand students' minds. The reverse occurs; students take positions that disallow disagreement. Is anyone left to wonder why Gen Z's views on social issues suddenly have cast many views of their parents as prejudiced and bigoted?

Along with the many excellent things that take place in education, others cause parents great concern. Parents have every right to question what happens at their child's school or college. Unlike previous generations, technology has made it easier for Gen Z to emote and buy into false premises and propaganda. Children invest emotion in things that easily can sidetrack them from their education.

The investment of a child's emotion and energy into something that is erroneous, outside the family's value structure, or is for the moment politically correct sometimes makes short shrift of the investment of their time. Anger is more easily provoked because of the instantaneous access to information and images that prompt emotion, sometimes superseding the facts. Crowd mentality can raise emotional levels to action levels, and these actions may be baseless. Emotions bring engagement, followings, and sometimes actions, but emotions do not necessarily bring accuracy and truth. Unlike previous generations, what ticks off people can very quickly spread by text message to assemble a mob seeking to vent its anger for various reasons.

Gen Z Character and Emotional Development

Mention the phrases "Gen Z teenagers" and "maturity" in the same breath—in the midst of a room full of adults—and watch the reactions. They will range from snickers to smiles, from groans to outright laughter. Has any parent of a teenager not been stymied by a response received from their child? Most parents of teenagers, at one time or another, have asked why they did "something," or said "those certain shocking words." Most parents easily can recall their teenagers' responses. The conversations probably went something like this:

> *Mom:* "Why did you do that?"
> *Daughter:* "Do what?"
> *Mom:* "Don't get flippant with me, young lady. Answer me!"
> *Daughter:* "I don't know."
> *Mom*: "What do you mean, 'you don't know?' Really? Well, you better think hard and come up with a good reason."
> *Daughter:* "I still don't know."
> *Mom:* "You're grounded."

If you are the average parent reading this fictional account, part of you thinks, "This kid knows exactly what she did." Yet, another part wonders whether that hopeless look in the face of questioning is genuine, and whether you did the right thing in grounding the teenager. *Welcome to teenage maturation*!

The field of neuroscience is providing answers to explain many typical teenagers' behaviors, such as the fictional account related here. It turns out that teenage impulsivity has its roots in brain development. Yes, teenagers have brains, despite rumors to the contrary. The frontal lobes of our brains are those areas where impulses are controlled. Scientists are telling us that the frontal lobes are not fully developed until well past the age of twenty—even twenty-five—according to some studies.

The different degrees of biological development for females and males have interesting implications for educators and parents. Teenage anger, joy, and sometimes tears for no apparent reason have their origin in parts of the teenager's brains. Gen Z parents might have heard their college daughters complain about the immaturity levels of young men their age. Many males, even into their early twenties, are not mature enough for females of the same age group. The brains of males mature more slowly, and differently.

Researchers William Hudspeth from Radford University and Kurt Fischer of Harvard Graduate School of Education have discovered that the average teen-ager's brain is still "wiring up," and certain growth spurts mark this wiring. They have determined three general periods of brain growth spurts: (1) between the ages of ten and twelve, (2) fourteen and sixteen, and (3) eighteen and twenty, although this may extend into the mid-twenties.

Barry and Murphy continue, as they address teenage impulsivity:

> Many people mix up impulsivity with risk-taking. In practice, they are quite different, particularly among adolescents. While the dopamine surge is critical to our understanding of risky behavior and pleasure-seeking, the manner in which the brain controls our impulsive behavior is different. The process of gradually gaining control of our impulsive behavior is a slow, linear one that occurs between the ages of thirteen and thirty. It is of great importance because the pathways of control come more from our logical prefrontal cortex back to our emotional brain than the reverse. One of the main pathways of control involves our serotonin cable, which is gradually maturing during this phase.[50]

Teenagers make various emotional connections in their brains, which is naturally the way most teenagers contextualize their world. Music places them somewhere. Parents can understand the place of music from their own past. An event categorizes a period in time, and music can recall this event. Whether romance, periods of tumultuous upheaval, of just periods of gleeful serenity, hearing songs from the past still evoke emotional reactions for adults. However, without context, where is the emotion?

Intrinsic Motivation

Intrinsic motivation may be a process emerging over time as a result of a stimulating environment that cultivates a child's curiosity or extends resident interests or abilities.[51] So what can teachers and parents do to encourage and stimulate growth of their students' internal motivation? *First*, parents and teachers must find ways to make certain what we are teaching is relevant. Students must see how their learning fits their world. *Second*, parents and teachers must provide good responses to the basic queries presented: "Why do we have to learn this stuff?" and "When are we ever going to use this in the real world?"

The answers to these two questions have been simplified. To the first question, the reply is *brain research shows that you need this in order to continue on to cognitive and emotional maturity*. They will stare into the distance, as with a glazed countenance, providing the very rationale needed. To the second, the answer as to when *the stuff* will be used in the real world is *now*. What they understand is, *we are being graded.* Grades make things relevant to their worlds in a hurry, both cognitively and emotionally. Grades contextualize learning and often provide, for the majority of students, motivation to at least accomplish something.

Impulse Control

Very few children have a handle on impulse control. They often act without giving themselves time to think through or reflect on their actions ahead of time. Teenagers accentuate the need for impulse control. Some of them appear simply to act before thinking.

Teenagers seem to possess an abundance of passion and drive but lack the intuition and knowledge, in terms of when to back off and slow down.[52] Parents and teachers can help students learn to control impulses by providing opportunities such as discussion, journaling, and places to vent. In the "good old days," physical education was available to allow students opportunities to both vent and work on self-control. The playground was a learning experience for many. Long-term projects and menial work that children do not value, dismissing it as irrelevant to their lives, may help to delay gratification, induce some self-discipline, and even cause necessary self-reflection.

Empathy

Empathy is an important aspect of a balanced emotional intelligence (EQ). Empathy also emerges from processes taking place in children's developing frontal lobes. Empathy allows students to act in ethical ways and to demonstrate altruism. High schools and even junior highs are requiring many hours of community service in order to assist in the development of empathy. Teachers can help by allowing students to share their thoughts and allow their expressions to connect with those of others. These expressions must be tempered at all times with proper classroom decorum. Writing is a way for a student to express even the more bizarre of thoughts that come to her. Parents and teachers should partner toward improving children's empathy.

Social Competence

Social competence allows students to "read" social contexts and respond adequately. This area and the area of empathy often are challenged by students participating in social media networks. Many older children and teenagers appear socially awkward, particularly when singled out or in budding relationships. This is why they find identity by resembling their friends in attire, hairstyle, taste in music, youthful language, and a variety of other points of connection. Technology, for Gen Z, provides a very easy point of identification and connection.

Pulitzer Prize–winning author and child psychiatrist Robert Coles writes: "Many of the options available to the young come at them not from within (the pressure of instinct, of desire, fueling a search for expression) but from without (social and cultural possibilities from a consumerist society ever ready to pester, entice, seduce and audience, an 'age group'). Young people, to repeat, take in values from the world, from the music they hear, the movies and television they see, from the fashion, advertising, and magazine industries as they influence what gets worn, what gets said, how hair is cut or colored, what hobbies are pursued."[53]

Gen Z's personal behaviors and manners come by conventional wisdom, in that these are more caught by young people who are taught how to behave; they do not come naturally from within.[54] Parents do much of this teaching. This has not changed much over the years. But the voices of culture seem much stronger today because children can be surrounded by these voices all day and all night, if they so choose. Maybe this is why parents of Gen Z have taken on a slightly different role with their children. Rather than helicopters, parents are taking much different roles, as protectors and guardians of the direction they see for their children.[55]

Parents, Not Buddies

Parents today are more likely to be parents than good buddies, or even elevated to the likability of a celebrity. Making certain their children get their fair share, or assuring the outcomes desired are achieved, parents then become a different sort of hero to their Gen Z children.[56] They have taken parenting in different directions. However, does this mean parents are missing key elements by their new approach?

Corey Seemiller of the University of Arizona's Leadership program writes the following about Gen Z: "Because of the power of social networking and the Internet, they are incredibly aware of what is going on around them in the world. . . . They are incredibly connected in that sense, and are more aware there are a lot of social justice issues and other deep-seated problems. . . . They have to have an emotional connection to a problem and feel like they are addressing the problem, not the symptoms. I see this as a generational shift. They want it to count for something; they want to delve much deeper into the problem."[57] They do this in the face of less optimism for their future compared to previous generations.[58]

Education researchers have to question whether Seemiller's observations of Gen Z mean that students come already with this package of concerns as part of their nature, or whether these concerns have been placed on them by the public education system and their families, changed at college through direct and indirect instruction by their professors, teachers, and parents.

Seemiller is correct, in that for Gen Z young people, engaging the emotions prompts actions. Actions have become more important to Gen Z than even the larger context, whether these actions are based in truth, falsehoods, or whether people are being used as pawns for attention to a cause associated with outcomes of another sort. Parents have backed into this reality by demonstrating to their children that acting quickly on something on their behalf is the new parenting paradigm.

As with all generations, the younger the person, the more she can be swayed easily by her emotions. No one should be surprised that emotions and Gen Z actions are inexorably tied. Gen Z is barely into their second and third decades of life. This means their brains are still developing and, along with this development, come emotions and reasoning. With this is mind, Barry and Murphy raise the issue of stress and its connection to anxiety and depression:

> If we grow up in an environment which encourages the stress box to be constantly overactive—such as a very anxious, perfectionistic, deprived or abusive house—we will develop pathways by adulthood which predispose us to anxiety. When real-life pressures come, as they inevitably will, those of us with short versions of the gene will have hypersensitive stress boxes that are easily sent into "overdrive." This causes a huge outpouring of glucocortisol, which can lead to an increased risk of developing anxiety/depression. Those of us with the long versions are less at risk. They seem also to ruminate less about the potential negative possibilities major stress might be about. Many feel that this is the main difference between the two groups.[59]

Penchant for Virtual Reality

Gen Z loves online games and fictional anime characters. A certain risk-taking associated with video gaming brings out emotional reactions, a near-perfect alignment of stress and frustration for the brains of Gen Z.

> Like Tezuka's anime characters, who were kids capable of harnessing the sometimes terrifying applications of technology, the children of the famous rubber-suited monster movies, too, were the only people capable of understanding the inner struggles and gentle natures of Godzilla, Mothra, and kiddie favorite Gamera. The monsters themselves were mostly the mutant result of nuclear accidents or toxic spills. The kids, because of their innocence, could communicate empathetically with the monsters, sing to them, and to some extent control their emotions. Kids could even persuade monsters to help save Tokyo from alien invasions or other disasters. Adults accidentally create monsters and catastrophes by letting their technology get out of control, while the children—thanks to their ability to understand the secret workings of technology and the secret hearts of monsters—are uniquely qualified to clean up the mess.[60]

Rushkoff writes: "Whenever new technology arrives, we learn the true nature of its predecessor. . . . The emergence of digitally stored and electronically distributed data has made old-fashioned printed media much more valuable to us. The fact that we can read text on our computer screens changed our perception of objects like books and magazines."[61] Rushkoff adds:

> Moreover, the time a child spends in the Pokemon craze amounts to a remedial lesson in how to consume. Pokemon teaches them how to want things that they can't or won't actually play with. In fact, it teaches them how to buy things they

don't even want. While a child might want one particular card, he needs to purchase them in packages whose contents are not revealed. He must buy blind and repeatedly until he gets the object of his desire. Worse yet, the card itself has no value—certainly not as a play thing. It is a functionless purchase, slipped into a display case, whose value lies purely in its possession. . . . Children are no longer playing. They are investing.[62]

"The Internet's unexpected social side effect turned out to be its incontrovertible main feature. Its other functions fall by the wayside. The Internet's ability to network human beings is its very lifeblood. It fosters communications, collaboration, sharing, helpfulness, and community."[63] As a result, "The Internet fostered a do-it-yourself mentality. We called it 'cyber-punk.'"[64] As the parent of a millennial/Gen Z child, the investing of emotions in the online world became all too real. The Pokemon craze led to the creation of an app, by a family member, that enhanced the geo-location and chat aspects of the game. This author, from personal experience, is well aware of the ability of the Internet to work human beings on deeply emotional levels.

Parents Take Heed

So, your Gen Z child is not interested in sports but lives to play online games. There is a caution for Gen Z parents in acquiescing to children's desires to rescue them from physical activity. Sitting around too much can cause issues for the developing brain. "Exercise has many positive effects in the brain. . . . The message here for parents is to try to involve your children in any form of sport or exercise from as early an age as possible. . . . Thirty minutes of brisk exercise three to five times a week is ideal. . . . The preference, though, would always be for aerobic exercise and, if possible, team sports."[65]

GEN Z STUDENT SURVEY

In order to ascertain specifics about Gen Z children/students, the following survey was conducted and shared in public and private school classrooms and homeschools across several states. The survey was strictly optional, and the names of the states have been omitted in order to ensure the highest level of privacy.

The idea behind the survey was to probe the minds and hearts of several hundred Gen Z students to collect their thoughts and feelings. A parent survey was taken and included in a previous chapter. Although it is possible that some parents and students are from the same families, no correlation is assumed between the parent data and the student data. The two surveys were offered approximately two months apart and were distributed to different groups.

The Survey

Four hundred sixty-two Gen Z students, ages fourteen to twenty-two, were surveyed. Public school and homeschool parents from around the nation shared a Survey Monkey link with students and assisted in the distribution of the survey.

The ten survey questions are listed next, along with the percentages of students responding to the choices. Some of the more poignant differences found within the responses are included. Students also were given two opportunities to include free responses, and many did so. Several of the more interesting responses are shared as well.

Here are the questions and responses:

1. *When were you born?*

    Ninety-four percent of the students who took the survey were born between 1998 and 2000. Another 4 percent selected the range 1995–1997; 2 percent were born between 2001 and 2003.

2. *What is your gender?*

    Of the Gen Z students who took the survey, 47 percent were male; 53 percent, female.

3. *How would you rate your use of smartphone technology?*

    All students surveyed had a smartphone. Thirty-six percent said they used their smartphone occasionally, or as needed. Sixty-four percent responded that their smartphones were such a regular part of their lives that they joke about having become addicted to them.

4. *Do you post on any social media sites?*

    Only 3 percent responded that they do not post on any social media sites. Seventeen percent claim to post on several social media sites throughout an average day, whereas 80 percent of the students replied that they post on one or more social media sites occasionally throughout an average day.

5. *How would you rate your digital literacy?*

    Digital literacy was broken into three categories. First, 83 percent claimed to be *digital natives*, which means they claim to understand digital technology and have been familiar with computers, smartphones, and the Internet from an early age. Second, 17 percent claimed to be *digital immigrants*. A digital immigrant is a person who has become familiar with computers, smartphones, and the Internet within the past one to three years. The last category was *digital foreigner*. Only seven of 462 students (.02 percent) responded that they know what smart technology is and that they even have a smartphone, but they are not well versed in how to use it.

6. *List three things that frustrate you about the generations that came before you.*

The question elicited 302 free responses given anonymously, without regard to age or gender. Some of the more interesting and poignant responses, which run the gamut, follow:

- They passed along their debt to us.
- Millennials are allowing socialism.
- Baby boomers ruined our economy, and now I am in debt for the rest of my life.
- Gen Xers do not understand us.
- Other generations think they know everything.
- Often they tease our generation for having our noses in our screens, but I see other generations doing it, and nothing is said.
- The 1990s were better than now, because we had more face-to-face interaction.
- Boomers are hyper-judgmental, especially of our work ethic.
- They have nothing other than conservative mind-sets.
- They expect us to adopt their ways of living and call us lazy for not doing so.
- Some of them are stubborn liberals.
- They talk about how difficult their lives were, when in reality we have different problems.
- They do not understand the competitiveness when applying to college.
- Previous generations treat us like children and then expect us to act like adults.
- They think all teenagers are the same in every generation.
- I get annoyed when I have to help my parents use their smartphones.
- Those other generations do not like change.
- My parents are far too overprotective.
- The previous generations were the ones with all the talent, and we are left with the scraps.
- Baby boomers are very strict.
- Millennials are very clique-oriented and do not make room for us.
- Previous generations are dumb and rude.
- People are mean, and there is no respect anymore.
- Economics have changed since the 1970s, and people need to understand this.
- Excessive enforcement of politically correct language limits freedom to speak our minds.
- Many blame the recent generation for problems, but it is every generation's fault.
- I am kind of envious that previous generations were able to afford things at earlier ages.

- Millennials think they are always right.
- Baby boomers are just annoying and overprotective.
- They cannot relate to a lot of modern issues regarding social and technological issues.

7. *As a Gen Z member, which of the following do you value the most?*

Listed in ascending order, Gen Z respondents claimed (1) 4 percent valued their technology the most, followed by two things other than those on the list (13 percent), (3) education (15 percent), (4) friends (16 percent), (5) their personal identity (20 percent), and (6) their parents (32 percent).

8. *Which of the following do you fear the most, in terms of your future?*

Slightly more than 9 percent of Gen Z students fear schooling. The category of "other" received approximately 11 percent. In addition, 17 percent of students had concerns about future relationships, 19 percent were worried about their future debt, and nearly 44 percent were worried about their future occupations. Picking up on this last response, the next question was meant for students to share their sense of optimism for future employment.

9. *How do you feel about the prospects of securing your dream job?*

Only 6 percent of Gen Z respondents were *not optimistic* about their future with respect to securing their dream jobs. Fifty-four percent were *guardedly optimistic* about the selection of their dream jobs, and 40 percent were *very optimistic* about their chances.

10. *List three suggestions that would help to make education better for your generation.*

Here are several of Gen Z students' suggestions:

- More scholarships to make college more affordable.
- Include classes in high school that are based on students' dream jobs.
- Offer more options for career paths.
- Allow more open discussion about what we disagree on without calling us haters and racists.
- Change the curriculum to things that are more important to our futures.
- Teach material that we will use when we are adults.
- Math could use a shot in the arm that is not Common Core.
- Involve more technology in classes.
- Give less homework.
- Find teachers who care more about students.
- Make it easier for teachers to communicate with students while teaching the curriculum.
- Stop worrying about wrong things like dress codes.
- Stop labeling groups.
- Using modern technology to learn, rather than forcing us to put away the technology we have become accustomed to using.
- Be open to suggestions about learning new things in class.

- We know you are the ones with the degrees, and such, and know how to teach. But we are the ones who know how to connect and make the process of education go as smoothly as possible.
- Use computers more often.
- Bring back freedom of speech and stop catering to the whining, marginal groups.
- Take away our phones. Make us read something for once. Make it mandatory to take "preparation for life" class.
- Don't call on me in class.
- More respect should be shown to authorities, especially teachers.
- Don't allow so much cell phone use in class. More one-on-one with teachers.
- Lower tuition.
- Find ways to reduce the rampant, spiraling costs of education.
- Reform the K–12 education system in America.
- Put better teachers in poverty-stricken areas.
- Don't forget about the higher-achieving students.
- Stop letting the federal government corrupt the education system in America.
- Have a class specifically for explaining things that come with adult life.

CONCLUSION

Gen Z parents should be aware of many things that affect the brain development and maturity of their children. Technology plays a large role in affecting the emotions of Gen Z children. Some of the things that make Gen Z tick are found in a sense of purpose and social causes. Social networking and continuous access to friends online are mainstays of Gen Z.

As teenagers, Gen Z goes through myriad changes in their personalities and behaviors. These are brain-based and, although challenging to parents, should be understood within the contexts within which they present themselves. At college, Gen Z is being exposed to various paradigms that insert themselves into the emotional makeup of older teenagers and young adults. Some of what makes Gen Z ticked comes as a result of exposure to groups that align themselves with social causes, and they seek to avoid being harmed by words and some of the beliefs of dissenting groups.

Gen Z students would be best served if they were allowed to experience the results and consequences of some of their own choices and fall short of their parents' expectations. Gen Z parents can frustrate their children when they step in to assist them in avoiding failure. This is clear from several of the comments elicited from the Gen Z student survey, as well as from the literature review. The future is bright for Gen Z, and it will be exciting to see the direction their accomplishments take the nation.

NOTES

1. Harry Barry and Edna Murphy, *Flagging the Screenager: Guiding Your Child through Adolescence and Young Adulthood* (Dublin, Ireland: Liberties Press, 2014), 25.

2. Denise Hawkins, "Here Comes Generation Z. What Makes Them Tick?" *NEA Today*, July 13, 2015. http://neatoday.org/2015/07/13/here-comes-generation-z-what-makes-them-tick/. Retrieved June 11, 2016. Cf. William McDonough and Michael Braungart, *Cradle to Cradle: Remaking the Way We Make Things* (New York: Farrar, Straus & Giroux, 2002), 109, 115, and 155.

3. Diane Smith and Monica Nagy, "Meet the Class of 2018: Digitally Fluent Gen Z," *Star-Telegram*, September 1, 2014. http://www.star-telegram.com/news/local/education/article3871560.html. Retrieved June 14, 2016.

4. "Generation Z and Money Survey: Understanding Tomorrow's Investors," *Ameritrade*, June 20, 2012. http://s1.q4cdn.com/959385532/files/doc_news/research/Gen ZandMoneyFindingFINAL-standard.pdf. Retrieved June 27, 2016. Cf. Hadley Malcolm, "Generation Z Worries about Paying for College, Getting a Job," *USA Today*, June 20, 2012. http://usatoday30.usatoday.com/money/perfi/basics/story/2012-06-19/generation-z-financial-habits/55694102/1. Retrieved June 27, 2016. Cf. also Shelly Kramer, "The Demographic Tsunami to Come: The Spending Habits of Gen Z," *Digitalist*, January 8, 2016. http://www.digitalistmag.com/customer-experience/2016/01/08/spending-habits-of-Gen Z-03927717. Retrieved August 5, 2016.

5. Gregory L. Jantz, "Brain Differences between Genders," *Psychology Today*, February 27, 2014. https://www.psychologytoday.com/blog/hope-relationships/201402/brain-differences-between-genders. Retrieved December 4, 2016. Cf. Kate Wheeling, "The Brains of Men and Women Aren't Really That Different, Study Finds," *Science Magazine*, November 30, 2015. http://www.sciencemag.org/news/2015/11/brains-men-and-women-aren-t-really-different-study-finds. Retrieved December 6, 2016.

6. "Generation Z: Digital Attention Deficit Disorder," *Mindshare*, August 12, 2014. http://www.mindshareworld.com/ireland/news/generation-z-digital-attention-deficit-disorder. Retrieved December 2, 2016.

7. Barry and Murphy, *Flagging the Screenager*, 41–42.

8. Caroline Leaf, "Cave Time Versus Chat Time: We Rest Differently," *Dr. Leaf*, September 15, 2011. http://drleaf.com/blog/cave-time-versus-chat-time-we-rest-differently/. Retrieved December 3, 2016.

9. Kenneth R. Ginsburg, "The Importance of Play in Promoting Healthy Child Development and Maintaining Strong Parent-Child Bonds," *American Academy of Pediatrics* 119(1) (January 2007): 182–91. http://pediatrics.aappublications.org/content/119/1/182. Retrieved December 5, 2016.

10. Barry and Murphy, *Flagging the Screenager*, 71.

11. Barry and Murphy, *Flagging the Screenager*, 73.

12. Michael S. Gazzaniga, *The Ethical Brain: The Science of Our Moral Dilemmas* (New York: HarperCollins, 2005), xviii.

13. Gazzaniga, *The Ethical Brain*, xix.

14. Alexandra Levit, "Make Way for Generation Z," *New York Times*, March 28, 2015http://www.nytimes.com/2015/03/29/jobs/make-way-for-generation-z.html?_r=0. Retrieved June 27, 2016.

15. Levit, "Make Way for Generation Z."

16. Levit, "Make Way for Generation Z."

17. Alex Williams, "Move Over, Millennials, Here Comes Generation Z," *New York Times*, September 18, 2015. http://www.nytimes.com/2015/09/20/fashion/move-over millennials-here-comes-generation-z.html?_r=0. Retrieved June 11, 2016.

18. Williams, "Move Over, Millennials."

19. Nancy Breiling Nessel, "Six Trends among Gen Z," *Getting Gen Z*, November 23, 2015. https://gettinggenz.com/2015/11/23/six-trends-among-generation-z-in-2016/. Retrieved June 26, 2016.

20. Williams, "Move Over, Millennials." Cf. William G. Ross, "Environmental Challenges Facing Generation Z," *Institute for Emerging Issues*, January 2013. https://iei.ncsu.edu/wp-content/uploads/2013/01/Environmental-Response.pdf. Retrieved August 4, 2016.

21. Levit, "Make Way for Generation Z."

22. Daniel Goleman, *Social Intelligence: Beyond IQ, Beyond Emotional Intelligence* (New York: Random House, 2007), 83.

23. Adam Renfro, "Meet Generation Z," *EdTech Getting Smart*, December 5, 2012. http://gettingsmart.com/2012/12/meet-generation-z/. Retrieved August 4, 2016.

24. Levit, "Make Way for Generation Z."

25. Emily Anatole, "Generation F: Rebels with a Cause," *Forbes*, May 28, 2013. http://www.forbes.com/sites/onmarketing/2013/05/28/generation-z-rebels-with-a-cause/#619669886aa1. Retrieved August 5, 2016.

26. Katherine Timpf, "Tutors: Girls May Be Made Too Upset by Microaggressions to Succeed on the SAT; They're Just Too Overrun with Emotion," *National Review*. June 27, 2016. Retrieved June 27, 2016. http://www.nationalreview.com/article/437200/tutors-girls-may-be-too-upset-microaggressions-succeed-sat.

27. Cheri Lucas, "Should Students and Teachers Be Online 'Friends'?" *Education.com*, July 2, 2009. http://www.education.com/magazine/article/Students_Teachers_Social_Networking/. Retrieved June 30, 2016.

28. Timpf, "Tutors: Girls May Be Made Too Upset by Microaggressions to Succeed on the SAT."

29. George Will, "College Kids Are Proving Trump's Point," *New York Post*, November 20, 2016. http://nypost.com/2016/11/20/college-kids-are-proving-trumps-point/. Retrieved November 21, 2016.

30. Sarah Brown, "A Brief Guide to the Battle over Trigger Warnings," *Chronicle of Higher Education*, August 26, 2016. http://www.chronicle.com/article/A-Brief-Guide-to-the-Battle/237600. Retrieved August 27, 2016.

31. Jonathan Haidt, "The Coddling of the American Mind," *The Atlantic*, September 2015, 16. http://www.theatlantic.com/magazine/archive/2015/09/the-coddling-of-the-american-mind/399356/. Retrieved June 22, 2016.

32. Haidt, "The Coddling of the American Mind," 16.

33. Fernanda Zamudia-Suarez, "Can Colleges Train Professors to Steer Clear of Microaggressions?" *Chronicle of Higher Education*, November 3, 2016. http://www.chronicle.com/article/Can-Colleges-Train-Professors/238289. Retrieved November 3, 2016.

34. Tyler O'Neil, "How C. S. Lewis Predicted Today's College Campus Craziness—in 1944," *PJ Media*, December 2015. https://pjmedia.com/faith/2015/12/1/how-c-s-lewis-predicted-todays-college-campus-craziness-in-1944/. Retrieved June 30, 2016.

35. Brown, "A Brief Guide to the Battle over Trigger Warnings."

36. Brown, "A Brief Guide to the Battle over Trigger Warnings."

37. Haidt, "The Coddling of the American Mind."

38. Haidt, "The Coddling of the American Mind."

39. O'Neil, "How C. S. Lewis Predicted Today's College Campus Craziness—in 1944."

40. Alexandra Levit, "The Future of Education According to Generation Z," *Time*, April 6, 2015. http://time.com/3764545/future-of-education/. Retrieved July 18, 2016.

41. Barry and Murphy, *Flagging the Screenager*, 52.

42. Barry and Murphy, *Flagging the Screenager*, 78.

43. Barry and Murphy, *Flagging the Screenager*, 52–53.

44. Patrick Deneen, "Professor Patrick Deneen Explains How Kids Have Become a Generation of Know-Nothings," *Signs of the Times*, February 2, 2016. https://www.sott.net/article/312948-Professor-Patrick-Deneen-explains-how-kids-have-become-a-generation-of-know-nothings. Retrieved July 7, 2016.

45. Deneen, "Professor Patrick Deneen Explains."

46. Deneen, "Professor Patrick Deneen Explains."

47. Peter Hawkins and Lucinda Schmidt, "Gen Z: Digital Natives," *Essential Kids*, July 18, 2008. http://www.essentialkids.com.au/life/technology/Gen Z-digital-natives 20080716-3g5p. Retrieved August 24, 2016.

48. Anne Kingston, "Get Ready for Generation Z," *Maclean's*, July 15, 2014. http://www.macleans.ca/society/life/get-ready-for-generation-z/. Retrieved August 24, 2016.

49. Kingston, "Get Ready for Generation Z."

50. Barry and Murphy, *Flagging the Screenager*, 68.

51. Robert Sylwester, *How to Explain a Brain: An Educator's Handbook of Brain Terms and Cognitive Processes* (Thousand Oaks, CA: Corwin Press, 2013). Cf. Robert Sylwester, *A Child's Brain: Understanding How the Brain Works, Develops, and Changes during the Critical Stages of Childhood* (New York: Skyhorse Publishing, 2013).

52. Barbara Strauch, *The Primal Teen: What the New Discoveries about the Teenage Brain Tell Us about Our Kids* (New York: Random House, 2003).

53. Robert Coles, *The Moral Intelligence of Children* (New York: Random House, 1997), 164.

54. Robert Sylwester, *The Adolescent Brain: Reaching for Autonomy* (Thousand Oaks, CA: Corwin Press, 2007).

55. Dan Schawbel, *Promote Yourself* (New York: St. Martin's Griffin, 2013), 171–76.

56. Corey Seemiller, "Trending Now: Generation Z," *Leadership Programs at the University of Arizona*, November 8, 2013. http://leadership.arizona.edu/. Retrieved June 26, 2016. Cf. La Monica Everett-Haynes, "Trending Now: Generation Z," *University of Arizona News*, November 8, 2013. https://uanews.arizona.edu/blog/trending-now-generation-z. Retrieved June 26, 2016.

57. Seemiller, "Trending Now"; Everett-Haynes, "Trending Now."

58. Seemiller, "Trending Now"; Everett-Haynes, "Trending Now."

59. Barry and Murphy, *Flagging the Screenager*, 82–83.

60. Douglas Rushkoff, *ScreenAgers: Lesson in Chaos from Digital Kids* (Cresskill, NJ: Hampton Press, 2006), 51–52.

61. Rushkoff, *ScreenAgers*, 79–80.

62. Rushkoff, *ScreenAgers*, 194.

63. Rushkoff, *ScreenAgers*, 206.

64. Rushkoff, *ScreenAgers*, 207.

65. Rushkoff, *ScreenAgers*, 85–86.

4

Gen Z and Their Technology

> Minecraft was designed with the main principle of building a community, in order for the game to be interesting, you play multi player. There is a heavy focus on engagement with . . . friends and cousins across the world. . . . The game was made for Generation Z because it is cultivating collaborative and intellectual stimulation [*sic*].[1]

GEN Z: A GLOBAL GENERATION

Does the possibility still exist for a family to stop at a restaurant, attend an athletic function, tour a museum, pass a bus stop, or even go to church without seeing a person on some sort of technology device? The answer is, "Probably not." Wherever you go, American culture is touched by the explosion of smart devices. And a higher concentration of devices is likely on school and college campuses, with an equivalent concentration of young people.

Gen Z shows little discretion as to where and when they use personal devices. Whether elementary, junior high, high school, or college, Gen Z is in love with technology. However, this adoration is not exclusive to American schools and campuses;[2] adults around the globe also have bought into the tech craze of the twenty-first century.

Unlike Gen Xers—who typically prefer talking on the phone to sending text messages—or millennials—who usually consider cell phones a part of their lives—Gen Z has its own set of technology preferences: shorter written communications and faster-paced personal messaging. In terms of having access to personal devices, Gen Z is different from other generations as well: they are more likely to have their first cell phone while in elementary school and view it as essential.[3]

Smart Device Discretion

Gen Z is more likely to view smartphones and smart technology as acceptable in any and all social settings. Compared to previous generations, Gen Z has seen others' privacy invaded, which is why, as a rule, they are more likely to avoid online transactions—with one exception. Gen Z esteems its smart apps and is increasingly and willingly using them for ease of organization and time management, and experimentally for financial management.[4]

In terms of messaging apps, Gen Z prefers to hide things and chooses to be diligent in its exercise of privacy. In part, this stems from the natural inclination of teenagers and young adults toward keeping things hidden from their parents and other adults. And privacy is part of the generational difference between millennials and Gen Z. Millennials tend to love social media platforms and the notoriety they bring. Gen Z typically chooses "messaging apps that don't leave a paper trail, where communications are sent and then are quickly gone, as users move on to the next stream of communication."[5]

The bottom line is this: Gen Z would rather communicate with people through their devices and play games against others than sit for an hour and converse, or play a board game in a smaller, in-person group.[6] How many adults have observed Gen Z children sitting next to each other and sending text messages and videos to each other, while laughing and critiquing as they do? Their medium is their new "me."

SMARTPHONE ADDICTION: IS IT REAL?

The ubiquitous presence of cell phones signals the profound nature of the digital age. It is here and it is not going away. One does not have to look around for long to see people of all ages on their cell phones. Earbuds are plugged in, heads are down, and people are in their own digital worlds. Many are unwilling to make eye contact at all.

From gymnasiums to schools, at bus stops and in automobiles, technology has touched every corner of the nation and the world. Gen Z has access to the entire world through its connectivity. In fact, as Torocsik, Szucs, and Kehl conclude, "Generation Z is the first global generation in the world"[7] and is given the phrase "Homo Globalis"[8] to signify this reality.

Teenagers tune out their parents much more easily today, which also means fewer confrontations. At the gym, teenagers constantly check their phones for text messages, toggling between Spotify and Pandora tunes. Between classes, thumbs blaze across smartphone touch screens. Others bounce to their downloaded music in stores and walking to and from destinations. Today more than ever, people with smart technology focus on themselves and temporarily shut out the rest of the world. This reality concerns educators and counselors.

One concern is about the effect of smartphones upon families. Another is about devices distracting attention from those behind the wheel and pedestrians crossing streets. Family safety concerns have arisen, but few are addressing Gen Z technology use and these concerns consistently. Parents drive their children to school, travel from the suburbs to the cities, all the while talking on their phones. Schools, law enforcement, churches, and community groups should join together to remind parents about the issue of safety. Gen Z and its parents are swept up in the modern age of infotainment and social communication.

Non-Talking Relationships

Children are entertained and kept quiet as they focus on video players and headsets in their family cars. Parents are in their own world, as they sit behind the wheel. What is equally concerning is that the rest of the family is *virtually* in another universe. The question for parents is: How is this new dynamic affecting relationships? What should be of enormous concern is the lack of depth of communication between people as a result of this new phenomenon. Parents should question the effect smartphones and devices have on the developing brains and general learning of their Gen Z children. Are parents concerned enough about possible long-term effects?

Smartphone access certainly is not limited to the United States or those living in Western societies. The rapid proliferation of communications technology and the Internet has brought unintended consequences to many societies. Families around the globe are struggling with their children over their use of smart technology. Text messages are sent by the billions daily: between WhatsApp and Messenger, more than sixty billion. In many ways, the world seems to be a smaller place for today's children, bringing with it both good and bad elements.

The Internet is both immediate and tantalizingly tempting, advantageous and detrimental over time. In the midst of all of the technological advancement of the twenty-first century, parents must question its effects upon their children.

Where Is the Depth?

Children in America and Europe seem to ask fewer questions of their parents, choosing instead to Google. While American families are motoring about the roadways, maybe for the first time in automobile history, the passenger children are quiet for long periods of time. How can this be such a bad thing for parents? Children are quiet because they are preoccupied. Their attention is diverted to in-vehicle monitors, earbuds, and smartphones. They play games and music on various personal devices, accessing Wi-Fi at their pleasure. Parents must guard against the practice that busyness equals substantive activity.

The attention span of Gen Z younger children has grown shorter because they are able to find information more quickly, and with much less analysis and critical thinking required. Understanding difficult academic concepts or questions about life often is not possible through the Internet; children do not come to understand who they are as persons or learn difficult concepts without parental intervention. Parents teach their children many of these ideas by words and actions, leaving us to wonder what children are *not* learning due to limited interaction with their parents.

Window of Opportunity

The good news is that younger Gen Z children are now asking their parents to reconnect with them and offer attention, despite their personal devices. They want to relate, yet keep their smart devices. But the window of opportunity for these connections is open for a short time. With the onset of the teenage years, teenagers' focus shifts away from parents as they bury themselves in countless apps on innumerable devices, staying strictly associated with peer groups. Starting in 2010, and going forward, it has become a reality for students who own their own cell phones: "the mobile phone has become the favored communication hub for the majority of teens."[9] This will only increase over time, further challenging families and relationships.

Parents, Please Take Heed

One 2015 study in England demonstrated to researchers that children are being affected negatively by their parents' uses of devices. "The children were speaking to researchers about who uses digital gadgets the most in their family home, and how it makes them feel. Two little girls say that their dad doesn't listen to them when he's on his phone and they have to repeat themselves, while one girl says: 'My mum spends all day on her computer and I feel sad because I won't get to play with her on a board game or something.'"[10] Children are sensing the ever-increasing disconnect within families, and these disconnects are more universal than first imagined.

A Little Comparison

Just a few decades ago, parents of baby boomers struggled with various problems with their children. Today, baby boomers and Gen Xers struggle over concerns with personal devices. The same is true with every generation that grows up and produces the next cohort. Struggles and clashes are inevitable. In the words of boxing legend George Foreman, raising children points out adult flaws superbly and makes hypocrites of many parents.[11]

The old adage *do as I say and not as I do* rings hollow in the ears of children, especially when their ears are plugged by earbuds. All things considered, this is life, and children had better get used to being disappointed.[12] However, the pressing question remains: How will children learn the deeper skills necessary for adulthood if parents are their ultimate situational saviors?

Turn Down What Music?

What baby boomer can forget agitated parents raising their voices above the din of rock music as it blared from stereos in their children's bedrooms? In the 1960s and 1970s, the only device baby boomers could take with them was a battery-powered transistor radio. Parents today complain that they have to yell louder and more often than their own parents did, just to attract their children's attention. Music is playing but only to the listener. The number of traffic accidents caused by baby boomers probably was not related to holding transistor radios to their ears—especially when what was being listened to also was available on the car radio.

Today, Gen Z is susceptible to driving accidents due to using their devices while behind the wheel of their car. Children are injured and killed while walking or riding their bikes in front of traffic they do not hear or see. The time spent looking down at their device screens does not lead to increased safety; the evidence is clear that Gen Z is placing itself in more precarious situations challenging their safety as they focus on their devices. This phenomenon is now referred to as *tech-neck*.

The Problem Is Within Reach

The students of Gen Z "reach for a smart device every 7 seconds."[13] Psychologists are catching up with what educators, and now concerned parents, have suspected for a long time: Gen Z appears addicted to smart technology. Now, the jury is out as to whether "addiction" literally means human brains are habitually and emotionally dependent upon their technology. But anecdotal evidence concludes that children must have a fix of technology, or someone might be on the receiving end of a terrible tantrum.

The literature on Gen Z focuses more on the attributes of the generation as they relate to smart technology addiction, particularly cell phones. What Gen Z parent has not experienced a child's complete emotional meltdown when something she wanted was taken away?

Some of these tantrums have occurred in public when children are asked to put away their devices or turn them off. These incidents—and more—have been recorded in classrooms; students have even become violent when their cell phones have been confiscated. But is anecdotal evidence enough to validate true addiction across a generation?

It remains unclear whether the anger and tantrums some children display when their devices are taken away are withdrawals from addiction or just impulses. They could be both. Gen Z would argue that we are all addicted to life, to eating and drinking, and other things. So, they ask, what is so terrible about an addiction to devices? This is a good question, and it is worth a good response.

WHAT IS SO TERRIBLE ABOUT DEVICE ADDICTION?

Gen Z cannot recall any time in their lives when communications and social media technology (smart phones) have not been a part of their lives.[14] Why was it that televisions and telephones, although popular, did not command the same attention as technology commands today? Could it be because telephones and televisions were stationary and much more easily monitored? Is it because smart technology became transient and portable, and became associated with human need as well as a social accessory?

British physician Dr. Harry Barry, a specialist in mental health, depression, and anxiety, shares an interesting observation and very revealing conclusion about Gen Z and its affection for technology: "The term 'screenager' . . . so perfectly describes our kids' age. Our teenagers and young adult are so immersed in the world of technology that many of them are struggling to separate their online worlds from real life. To ignore the impacts of technology and social media on how our adolescents are developing would be foolish."[15] Barry raises an excellent point. Today's teenagers struggle with separation of their online world and the real world.

Younger Gen Z users probably are more concerned about people discovering their social media communication and photo posts than they are about losing their technology privilege for a time. In an age when the government has spied on many of us, and our private records have been compromised by IRS and NSA scandals, today's older students have very little fear of invasion of privacy, thereby putting out more information about their lives and beliefs on the Internet.

Social media users spend a "great deal of time"[16] on their pages, posting the latest happenings. They are certain everyone wants to know where they are, what they are doing, and view the best photo possible. Perhaps the central question for any younger user of today's social media is captured in the curious query, "What are my friends doing and saying now?"[17]

Nevertheless, "as most family doctors, therapists and parents know . . . the most vulnerable years are between eighteen and twenty-five."[18] These years probably are the most significant for support and mentoring, because "the emerging adult has the greatest freedom and the least support."[19] Gen Z—the first of them born about 1995—soon will number in the dozens of millions.

Scientists and psychologists take many sides in this discussion, and studies are being performed annually, attempting to reach consensus about reliance and addiction. It is clear that reliance on smart technology is heavy. But Gen Z is not using their devices for voice communication; for them, mere talking on cell phones is becoming passé.

Heavy Reliance on Devices as Evidence of Addiction?

Heavy reliance on technology has led many researchers to conclude Gen Z is addicted to smart devices, the Internet, and online games. They cite statistics to bolster their case. More than 95 percent of teenagers between twelve and seventeen say they have an online presence, and 76 percent claim one or more social networking sites in their name. Seventy-seven percent of that age group surveyed acknowledged their ownership of cell phones. Contrast these statistics with those between eighteen and twenty-nine. Eighty-four percent admitted to using social networking sites regularly, and 97 percent have cell phones.[20]

According to researchers, technology addiction is real and is having a negative effect on students even at younger elementary age. Some argue that addiction is reaching into other generations, including the baby boomers.

According to researchers, device use affects brain development and behaviors in Gen Z teenagers. For example, it has been argued that students with ADHD often are more focused with the use of technology. This may be true, as they are able to focus only on the technology. However, this focus is a distraction from other things of importance. Therefore, some contend that the very distractions minimized by device usage yield to other distractions, exacerbated by the use of technology. This exacerbation has led researchers to construct a new label for an old disorder: "AOADD: Always-On Attention Deficit Disorder."[21]

Gen Z's heavy reliance on smart technology is having a terribly disruptive effect on learning, behaviors, focus, and self-control in the classroom. A recent study by the Cranfield School of Management revealed that 39.3 percent of Gen Z preteens and teens surveyed admitted they used text shortcuts that had a deleterious effect on the quality of their writing.[22] Essentially, the use of texting, over time, diminished their English writing skills.[23]

Public school teachers in the United States certainly do not disagree that cell phone texting, Instagram, Snapchat, and Twitter have reduced the quality and depth of written expression, as well as face-to-face interaction. Gen Z, if nothing else, is heavily reliant on and obsessed with their devices and social media.

According to Andrew Kakabadse, Susan Bailey, and Andrew Myers, a recent study of 260 Midlands, United Kingdom, students ages eleven through eighteen produced some stark revelations: "technology obsession hinders spelling skills, implicitly encourages plagiarism, and disrupts classroom learning. Despite school policies restricting mobile phone usage, students use the phone frequently, with the majority making calls from the toilets. The mobile phone continues to be a prime channel of social communication during the school day."[24]

When it comes to parenting Gen Z in the era of smart technology, parents should remind themselves of a few things. First, the more time their children spend with devices, the more they become reliant on them. Moods and attitudes certainly are affected by children's heavy use. Second, analyze whether their children can put aside their devices without anger or emotion. Telltale signs of heavy reliance and addiction may overlap, and parents should make every effort to diminish a child's inordinate need for their device. Third, fight the tendency to minimize what they sense is addiction. It is better to be safe than sorry when it comes to children and their developing emotions and habits. Remember, when children spend hours online, they cannot remain focused on the original task if they switch their attention to another task.

Dr. Nicholas Kardaras, executive director of one of the nation's top addiction rehabilitation center, The Dunes East Hampton, writes about why parents and teachers are seeing increases in behavior issues and distractibility among students in schools: "Many parents intuitively understand that ubiquitous glowing screens are having a negative effect on kids. We see the aggressive temper tantrums when the devices are taken away and the wandering attention spans when children are not perpetually stimulated by the hyper-arousing devices. Worse, we see children who become bored, apathetic, uninteresting and uninterested when not plugged in."[25]

Gen Z parents must realize that teenagers will resist parents' attempts to restrict their device usage. Today, this resistance also is being observed in young children. An addict needs his or her fix. Removing a device may be as volatile as removing someone's cigarettes or drugs, because the brain area affected by the addiction is firing in dopamine, regardless the stimulus that triggers it. As evidence of addiction, Kardaras is quick to point out that parents see the *fix phenomenon* increasing among their teenagers. They cannot avoid touching and looking at their devices for more than a few seconds. Device addiction can be almost as bad as an addiction to heroin—at least the brain seems to think so.[26]

Assuming children are addicted to their devices, technology addicts will deny they have a problem and make all sorts of promises to assure parents they have things under control. So, regardless of age, the pressure will come at parents differently, based on emotional appeals, and needs for technology for grades and classes. In some incidents, the user has threatened personal bodily harm to both himself and the parent. Participating in today's technology, whether games, social media, or communication, amounts to "a form of digital drug."[27]

Heavy use of digital technology greatly affects the frontal cortex of the brain. This area controls executive functioning—as well as impulses. In fact, digital technology reacts in the brain "in exactly the same way that cocaine"[28] acts in the brain. This evidence has led UCLA director of neuroscience Peter Whybrow to refer to Internet addiction as "electronic cocaine."[29] Among those addicted and its heavy users, modern digital technology "is so hyper-arousing that it raises dopamine levels—the feel-good neurotransmitter and most involved in the addiction dynamic—as much as sex."[30]

A Recent Kaiser Study

The Kaiser Family Foundation convened a study in 2010 on the usage of digital communication and social media technologies. This study also included usage of smartphones. The group that participated in the study places them squarely in the middle Gen Z, with some of the subjects overlapping with millennials. The following is a summary of six of the results.[31]

1. Students, on average were multitasking, using one form or more of technology simultaneously while engaged in other tasks. Students averaged more than seven hours per day connected to their devices.
2. Students often chose technology over other activities, including physical exercise, schoolwork, jobs, and even face-to-face meetings with friends.
3. Most of the time students were either on their computers or their cell phones, often surrounded by other sights and sounds produced by other forms of technology, especially entertainment-oriented forms.
4. Social media sites were a prime focal point for up to one-half of the students surveyed, depending on the time of day.
5. Grades of students whose use of technology could be in the range of heavy reliance, or as some would determine, addictive, tumbled downward, and were of greater concern than those students whose usage was much less.
6. Total media exposure by race and/or ethnicity warrants further consideration in terms of implications for education. White students were exposed to more than eight hours of media a day; Hispanic and black students, some thirteen hours a day.

The brains of Gen Z are bombarded with more distracting stimuli than recent generations. Educators with any significant length of teaching experience will attest that most classrooms today have the appearance of addicts reaching for their substance, or looking for their fixes; Gen Z is emerging as the addiction generation with frightening implications for their brains. This is not just an issue for older teenagers and young adults. The younger members of "Generation Z have the same problems as the previous young generations did, but their technical opportunities provide such new frames in their lives which make their behavior incomprehensible for elderly generations."[32] But who should receive the blame for this technology-addicted generation?

Ironically, the reader should note the contrast between the people behind the inventions of the technology used today and its usage by their own families. It seems those parents who were the forerunners of what we term high-tech communications and games today knew something many others did not even consider. For example, Apple's "Steve Jobs was a notoriously low-tech parent. Silicon Valley tech executives and engineers enroll their kids in no-tech Waldorf schools. Google founders Sergey Brin and Larry Page went to no-tech Montessori schools, as did Amazon creator Jeff Bezos and Wikipedia founder Jimmy Wales."[33]

What message can parents take from this? If the inventors moderate tech usage for themselves and their families, what message does that send consumers?

ATTRACTIONS AND DISTRACTIONS

Since the Kaiser study, technology addictive behaviors have gotten worse. Schools are not helping students by permitting them to be wired up all day; parents of older Gen Z children probably are seeing an uptick in class assignments and homework that require Internet use.

Schools enable wireless connections directly in classes for students who bring their own devices, or for students whose devices are provided for them by schools. Clearly, nothing is wrong with technology per se. "It is here to stay whether we like it or not."[34] But the high rate of usage is causing serious physiological and psychosocial concerns, meaning its usage is much more than mere distractions.

If society continues to advance access to devices and expects education simply to succumb to these attractive advancements, a concern is that devices will cause greater distractions rather than improve learning. Eventually, they may lead to lasting "negative effects on the emotional, social and cognitive development of the brain and young persons."[35] Such effects may become more startling that just the inability of Gen Z to focus.

Noticing Changes

Parents should ask themselves whether they notice changes in their children when they take away a smart device as a form of discipline. One parent referred to a childhood memory and noticed a similarity from her own youth: "When I took away my teenager's cell phone, it was similar in reaction to the time I took away my mother's cigarettes. It's funny the things you remember from your youth."

Children today are dealing with more and more distractions caused by their technology at critical developmental periods for their brains to produce significant academic achievement. Parents should be wary of any technology that changes their children's behavior to the point where reliance on it takes the place of family, fun, and its incorporation into the daily regimen is uncompromised. This pertains to everything from regular online gaming all-nighters with friends to emotional upheavals over texting.

Smart technology is an embedded part of the emotions and psychological makeup of heavy users. For example, Gen Z has developed the tendency to allow their cell phones to interrupt their sleep patterns. This is critical for parents to understand: "During sleep, the brain secretes melatonin, making us drowsy, and generally switches off its serotonin and noradrenaline systems. On waking, melatonin levels fall, and the serotonin and noradrenaline systems switch on, making us alert."[36] When children are sleepy it means their brains are not firing on all cylinders, to use an automobile metaphor.

Barry and Murphy contend technology access during sleep hours is a regular interruption of growth and overall child development. Students' brain chemicals are switching on and off repeatedly throughout the night. "The average sleep cycle is eight hours, but we now know that adolescents and emerging young adults require up to nine and a half hours of sleep to function normally. . . . Since time immemorial, parents have struggled to get their adolescents and young adults in their early twenties out of bed in the morning and to bed at a reasonable time at night."[37] As educators can attest, there is no doubt today that students are *not* getting enough sleep.

GEN Z AND THEIR ZS

A commonsense recommendation for parents is to remove smartphones from children's rooms—even if they say they need them for the alarms. Suggest buying them an alarm clock and watch their reaction. Baby boomers' parents used the same logic with their children, once they caught onto the lyrics of some of the 1960s' and 1970s' songs. Many children during those years were very adamant that they only liked the music—the lyrics were just a sideshow.

Once parents began suggesting they could replace the rock albums with sound tracks that could meet the musical interest, the real reasons came forward. The same likely will be true among Gen Z if a parent suggests replacing a smartphone alarm with an alarm clock. If the child says, "You don't trust me," the parent should reply, "I trust you. And if you trust me, you'll give me your smartphone for the night."

"There is a lot to be said for insisting that smartphones be left in the living room and that Internet access is cut off after 11 PM at night. This will greatly increase the chance of the young person getting sufficient sleep, while also greatly reducing the risk of night-time cyberbullying,"[38] among other things.

A recent study by the University of California at San Francisco concluded that screen time on smartphones at certain times of the day, especially later in the evenings, impacts sleep patterns and leads to serious sleep deprivation.[39] Secondary teachers probably are nodding in agreement right now, reflecting on their first two periods of the day, when heads are plopped on desks, and hoodies are pulled up in warm protection from the classroom instruction.

The UCSF study concluded that for adults "total screen time averaged 38.4 hours per 30 days, and average screen time per hour was 3.7 minutes, equivalent to one hour 29 minutes per day."[40] Screen time for young people varied by their ages. However, the researchers reported that "longer average screen-time was associated with shorter sleep duration and worse sleep-efficiency. Longer average screen-times during bedtime and the sleeping period were associated with poor sleep quality, decreased sleep efficiency, and longer sleep onset latency."[41] In other words, falling asleep took longer, and remaining asleep became problematic with increased screen time near or at bedtime.

Cutting Corners

Spending too much time on the Internet socializing may result in viewing the larger nature of the Internet as of lesser importance. This may affect children's attitudes toward schoolwork and even ethics. Gen Z's cutting corners leads to more distractions, and technology that is relied upon to cut such corners has negative effects on span of attention and students' ability to focus academically.

It's So Easy

The ease of access to information on the Internet has produced a different perspective on cheating. Gen Z students which cut corners actually compromise their honesty, work ethic, and academic integrity. Kakabadse asserts, "A high proportion of teenagers (59.2%) admitted to inserting information straight from the internet into schoolwork, without actually reading or changing it. Almost a third (28.5%) deemed this as acceptable practice despite recognizing that such behavior is considered plagiarism."[42] A prevailing notion is that if something is on the Internet, it must be *free to me*. In the words of a former student, who stated calmly, "It's so easy to snag something from the Internet."

Attention Deficits and Smart Technology

Depending on the physicians and the diagnoses, the number of American students diagnosed with ADHD is in the millions and increasing at an alarming rate. Parents would be remiss to conclude that the high numbers of ADHD students stem only from a physiological problem from birth. That being said, the debate is ongoing about whether screen time on smartphones, computers, and big screen television causes ADHD, or makes it worse over time. Scientific research is ongoing to determine whether ADHD can be caused while children's brains are developing, or whether the condition becomes more complicated due to increased screen time.[43]

Parents used to sit their children in front of television sets as babysitters. Children were quiet while their favorite programs were broadcast. Today, parents hand their children iPads and smartphones, have large-screen televisions in their bedrooms for gaming adventures, so the babysitting has taken on an entirely new dynamic. What has this new dynamic caused in students already diagnosed with ADHD?

According to the organization Children and Adults with Attention-Deficit/ Hyperactivity Disorder (CHADD), "people with ADHD run a much higher risk of Internet addiction than neurotypicals—estimates run as high as twenty-five percent of the ADHD population. Such excessive screen-time use is associated with a multitude of problems. These include troubled relationships with families and friends, poor school/work performance, fatigue, and poor sleep."[44] Parents thought they were doing their ADHD child a favor when they sensed a new focus while she was using technology; now they realize that child is unable to deal with limiting or removing technology from his or her daily life.

ADHD also appears to be influenced by environmental factors, such as home and classroom structures, as well as by peers. The sensory distractions children face today far outweigh the distractions of previous generations. Older students now have little time to daydream. The moment they are bored, which seems more quickly than ever, the cell phone comes out, games are played, and messages are sent and received. Technology always seems to be begging for attention, but it only adds to the distractions or feeds a psychological compulsion.

Gen Z's Brain Candy

The majority of teenagers with short attention spans and processing issues are not willing to delay gratification. After all, the enticement of the device, working in tandem with immediate gratification and heightened flow of dopamine to the child's brain, creates the perfect psychological storm.[45] The frightening part is that the "vast majority of mental illness—75 percent actually appears for the first time when people are between the ages of thirteen and twenty-five."[46] Parents have to wonder to what extent their Gen Z children are in line to become a statistic.

The imbalance of emotions at certain ages, especially teenage years, made worse by overuse of technology, is cause for concern. There is a direct connection between brain development and "significant life stressors experienced during this critical period."[47] Technology for Gen Z seems to be *brain candy*. Parents are strongly encouraged to discover whether the correlation is significant between the explosion of students who have been diagnosed with learning disabilities, ADHD, and are behaviorally challenged and the increased proliferation of personal devices. Moreover, another question is whether there is a causal relationship between device usage and the worsening of disorders.

NEW TECHNOLOGIES AND LEARNING

The cognitive effects of modern technology upon student learning are being studied more deeply by researchers. Each year, newer and faster gadgets entice students away from developing essential people skills, reduce communication to a limited number of characters, and diminish writing and reading skills. Just ask any language arts teacher about the quality and level of his or her students. Watch any young person count change from a cash register.

In far too many schools in America today, students' ability to dig deeply into learning is sacrificed for shallow approaches to cognitive discoveries and fact-finding missions. The culprit that has been blamed for this shallowness is speed of access and supposed multitasking.[48] The faster the device, the shorter the patience and related attention span. The faster an answer is achieved, the less a person senses the need to dig more deeply. It is all so easy to play music in one ear, listen to cable television with the other—all while typing a phrase into a Google or Yahoo search.

Patience, or waiting for anything, is lost on Gen Z. Quick clicks bring several-seconds-long videos. Photos are snapped every few seconds. Texting friends while talking on the same phone make it easy to divide focal points. In the classroom, asking students to write anything of length has become a struggle. At home, monitoring children with various device distractions does little to increase the discipline and focus required for success at school.

Monitoring needs to graduate to removal at some point. We are now a nation of distracted learners, distracted drivers, and distracted in our relationships. Reversing the trend may be impossible, but modification can help to recover some focus.

The following is an example of how serious the addictive quality of smart devices has become. Even in classrooms and with multiple warnings, students are distracted by short-term memory deficits due to the tempting tugs of their phones. Threatened even with a failing grade if their cell phones come out in class, some students submit to their compulsion with technology. Teachers are struggling with classroom management issues today like never before.

Technology Affects Thinking

Barry and Murphy associate use of devices with concerns about student cognition. They also correlate technology use and effects on the areas of the brain required for deeper, long-term memory retention and associate their effects with technology use.[49] According to their research, modern technology inhibits students from taking time to think through ideas from start to finish and reduces the time required for in-depth critical analysis. Consequently, students take less time for quality analysis, relegating answers to the expertise and analysis of another, which is most often online just a click away.

This should be a wake-up call for parents and teachers. The use of smart technology at home and in the classroom should be monitored and managed to promote deepening learning. Children who seek answers to questions based on the principle that faster is better often will select the first link to something relevant online; and if they are taught that work comes before play, they should not be faulted when they finish their work as quickly as possible. Technology feeds that mind-set, and Gen Z is right in the middle of this trough.

At home, parents should lay out the aspects of the work required, and the details children must adhere to in order to satisfy the work requirements at home. Likewise, if students in the classroom, or in a homeschool situation, use the "first-link-click" method to deepen learning, then the depth of that learning in soon automated in the *reality of the shallow*. Children who finish their work quickly have not taken the time to reflect on much of anything, but they likely cannot wait any longer before they can play. Gen Z must be forced to delay its compulsion for speed and begin to develop broader critical-thinking skills.

SOCIAL MEDIA AND IMMEDIATE GRATIFICATION

Parents and teachers participate in it. Administrators are told to steer clear of it. Students are proficient in it. People date by it. America is taken by the social media reality, and it has become as much a part of the national psyche as the selfie—and not just any self-taken photo. Sometimes people put more thought into the type of photo to take with their smartphones than they do into their chores around the house or their schoolwork—or even into their real-world relationships. The immediate glorification of oneself supersedes many other aspects of American culture.

Take, for example, girls pouting and fish-lip puckers, posing postures, as if to promote something beyond their years. Students are not alone in self-promotion. Teachers post their own personal photos. Men and women take photographs in mirrors, at gymnasiums, in restrooms, and even from within much more intimate domains. Muscles, tight outfits, piercings, and tattoos are shown to the world from workout centers. Americans, in general, have become celebrants of everything. Family goings-on are posted. Updates on hospital visits and what was eaten for dinner are shared with a person's online world. Americans love themselves and think others want to celebrate this love with them.

Stop and think for a moment. Gen Z children have learned this behavior from somewhere. Immediate gratification extends to parents taking photos of themselves in cars or with friends. Police have resorted to body-cams to justify their actions on citizens' behalf. Snapchats and extended videos are found in newsfeeds and prompt the online user's curiosity. If a person wants to find a lover, a spouse, or plan an extramarital affair, social media is now the platform. Everyone can be a viral sensation or a critic, a bully, a narcissistic wonder, even the president of the United States.

Social media networking is now a daily necessity for most in Gen Z.[50] The upside is that parents at least are informed about their children's friends. However, the issue that is most worrisome is what will become of the masses over time. The satisfaction, however momentary, is no replacement for relational longevity and deeper human interactions. In fact, no selfie in the world can replace reality.

CONCLUSION

Those in Gen Z spend much more time on social media communications than most of their millennial counterparts.[51] They certainly spent more time online than Gen Xers and baby boomers. They spend most of this time socializing in ways previous generations did not or could not.[52] Equally true, it has become a serious and compulsive distraction for Gen Z.[53]

As younger children grow, parents must be more diligent and attentive to effects of the new age of technology on the overall health of their child. This includes their brains, their bodies, their personalities, and their skills with both people and things. Technology is not going away as the world gets more connected. The test for parents with their children is whether technology can be managed better, or whether a generation of addicts will be defined and accommodated in our nation's schools. The future is calling, but because Gen Z is already digitally engaged, will the call go to voicemail?

NOTES

1. Amanda Ashworth, "What Recruitment Can Learn from Minecraft and Gen Z," *Undercover Recruiter*, n.d. http://theundercoverrecruiter.com/recruitment-minecraft-gen -z/. Retrieved December 14, 2016.

2. Brian Mastroianni, "How Generation Z Is Changing the Tech World," *CBS News*, March 10, 2016. http://www.cbsnews.com/news/social-media-fuels-a-change-in-genera tions-with-the-rise-of-Gen Z/. Retrieved November 23, 2016.

3. Mastroianni, "How Generation Z Is Changing the Tech World."

4. Amy Levin-Epstein, "Get Ready for Generation Z at Work," *CBS News: Money Watch*, September 16, 2014. http://www.cbsnews.com/news/get-ready-for-generation-z -at-work/. Retrieved November 23, 2016.

5. Mastroianni, "How Generation Z Is Changing the Tech World."

6. Mastroianni, "How Generation Z Is Changing the Tech World."

7. Maria Torocsik, Kristin Szucs, and Daniel Kehl, "How Generations Think: Research on Generation Z," *Acta Universitatis Sapientiae, Communicatio* 1 (2014): 30.

8. Torocsik, Szucs, and Kehl, "How Generations Think."

9. Amanda Lenhart et al., "Teens and Mobile Phones," Pew Research Center, April 20, 2010. http://www.pewinternet.org/2010/04/20/teens-and-mobile-phones/#fn-440-1. Retrieved October 30, 2016.

10. Kirstie McCrum, "Children Reveal 'Hidden Sadness' of Parents Spending Too Much Time on Mobile Phones in Heartbreaking Video," *Mirror*, August 10, 2016. http:// www.mirror.co.uk/news/world-news/children-reveal-hidden-sadness-parents-6228329. Retrieved November 23, 2016.

11. George Foreman, *Fatherhood by George* (Nashville: Thomas Nelson, 2008).

12. Foreman, *Fatherhood by George.*

13. Tiffany Ford, "Five Tips for Teaching Gen Z in College," *Top Hat Blog*, November 25, 2015. https://blog.tophat.com/generation-z/. Retrieved October 22, 2016.

14. "Get Ready for Generation Z," *Robert Half International, Enactus*, 2015. https:// www.roberthalf.com/sites/default/files/Media_Root/images/rhpdfs/rh_0715_wp_genz_ nam_eng_sec.pdf. Retrieved June 27, 2016.

15. Harry Barry and Edna Murphy, *Flagging the Screenager: Guiding Your Child through Adolescence and Young Adulthood* (Dublin, Ireland: Liberties Press, 2014), 25.

16. Paul Taylor, *The Next America: Boomers, Millennials, and the Looming Generation Showdown* (New York: Public Affairs/Pew Research Center, 2015), 183.

17. Taylor, *The Next America: Boomers, Millennials, and the Looming Generation Showdown*, 183.

18. Barry and Murphy, *Flagging the Screenager*, 25.

19. Barry and Murphy, *Flagging the Screenager*, 25.

20. Janna Anderson and Lee Rainie, "Main Findings: Teens, Technology, and Human Potential in 2010," Pew Research Center, February 29, 2012. http://www.pewinternet .org/2012/02/29/main-findings-teens-technology-and-human-potential-in-2020/. Retrieved November 5, 2016.

21. Anderson and Rainie, "Main Findings."

22. "Technology Addiction Disrupts Teenage Learning," *Cranfield University Blog*, September 9, 2009. https://alumni.cranfield.ac.uk/public/News_Item.aspx?Id=661. Retrieved November 5, 2016.

23. "Technology Addiction Disrupts Teenage Learning."

24. "Technology Addiction Disrupts Teenage Learning."

25. Nicholas Kardaras, "It's Digital Heroin: How Screens Turn Kids into Psychotic Junkies," *New York Post*, August 27, 2016. http://nypost.com/2016/08/27/its-digital -heroin-how-screens-turn-kids-into-psychotic-junkies/. Retrieved August 31, 2016.

26. Kardaras, "It's Digital Heroin."

27. Kardaras, "It's Digital Heroin."

28. Kardaras, "It's Digital Heroin."

29. Peter Whybrow, "UCLA Faculty Voice: Neuroscience Helps Explain American Households' $12 Trillion Debt," *UCLA Newsroom*, May 15, 2015. http://newsroom.ucla .edu/stories/ucla-faculty-voice-neuroscience-helps-explain-american-households-12 -trillion-debt. Retrieved October 1, 2016.

30. Kardaras, "It's Digital Heroin."

31. "Generation M2: Media in the Lives of 8-to-18-Year-Olds," The Henry J. Kaiser Family Foundation, 2010. https://kaiserfamilyfoundation.files.wordpress.com/2013/04/8010 .pdf. Retrieved July 17, 2016.

32. Torocsik, Szucs, and Kehl, "How Generations Think," 30.

33. Kardaras, "It's Digital Heroin."

34. Barry and Murphy, *Flagging the Screenager*, 96.

35. Barry and Murphy, *Flagging the Screenager*, 96.

36. Barry and Murphy, *Flagging the Screenager*, 75.

37. Barry and Murphy, *Flagging the Screenager*, 75.

38. Barry and Murphy, *Flagging the Screenager*, 77.

39. Matthew A. Christensen et al., "Direct Measurements of Smartphone Screen-Time: Relationships with Demographics and Sleep," *Public Library of Science: PLOSone*, November 9, 2016. http://journals.plos.org/plosone/article?id=10.1371/journal .pone.0165331. Retrieved November 12, 2016.

40. Christensen, "Direct Measurements of Smartphone Screen-Time."

41. Christensen, et al., "Direct Measurements of Smartphone Screen-Time." Cf. Kathryn Doyle, "Smartphone Screen Time Tied to Lower Sleep Quality," *Bakersfield Californian*, November 12, 2016, A2.

42. "Technology Addiction Disrupts Teenage Learning," *Cranfield University Blog*.

43. Martin L. Kutscher and Natalie Rosin, "Too Much Screen Time? When Your Child with ADHD Over-Connects To Technology," *Children and Adults with Attention-Deficit/ Hyperactivity Disorder (CHADD)*, June 2015, 22–25. http://www.chadd.org/Attention PDFs/ATTN_06_15_TooMuchScreenTime.pdf. Retrieved November 12, 2016.

44. Kutscher and Rosin, "Too Much Screen Time? When Your Child with ADHD Over-Connects To Technology."

45. C. Kieling et al. "Neurobiology of attention hyperactive disorder," *PubMed: United States National Library of Medicine at the National Institutes of Health* 17(2) (April 17, 2008): 285–307.

46. Barry and Murphy, *Flagging the Screenager*, 25.

47. Barry and Murphy, *Flagging the Screenager*, 25–26.

48. Barry and Murphy, *Flagging the Screenager*, 98.

49. Barry and Murphy, *Flagging the Screenager*, 98–100.

50. Scarlet Madison, "Teens and the Cruel World of Social Networking," *Techi*, December 9, 2011. http://www.techi.com/2011/12/teens-and-the-cruel-world-of-social -networking/. Retrieved August 4, 2016.

51. Amanda Lenhart, "Teens, Technology and Friendships," Pew Research Center, August 6, 2015. http://www.pewinternet.org/2015/08/06/teens-technology-and-friendships/. Retrieved August 4, 2016.

52. "Teens' Cruel World of Social Media: Infographic," *Youth Ministry Media*, September 16, 2015. http://www.youthministrymedia.ca/infographics/teens-cruel-world-of -social-media-infographic/. Retrieved August 4, 2016.

53. Torocsik, Szucs, and Kehl, "How Generations Think," 30.

5
Partnering with
Parents for Gen Z Success

We were talking . . . of the generation of Facebook . . . You know some people call it Fakebook because you post happy pictures. You don't ever see a picture of a tantrum, a picture of where you are like, crying.[1]

Don't let anyone look down on you because you are young, but set an example . . . in speech, in life, in love, in faith, in purity.[2]

BUILDING COMMUNITY

Relationships are highly important to Gen Z. Family is intensely meaningful to American society, and Gen Z understands this and feels this deeply. They are quite interested in maintaining close connections with family, although sometimes they are unable to strike a balance between their compulsion with technology and their feelings for family. Feelings that fluctuate often are not the best measure by which to gauge relationships. Therefore, consider at least five factors in the establishment of relationships between Gen Z and their parents.

First, understand that Gen Z seeks unconditional acceptance. They are children of other generations, and do not want to be judged for their beliefs and behaviors. Gen Z is a softer generation and decries challenges to their beliefs. This is highly important, and relationship development has to take this into consideration. The reason it is so important is because they take personal challenges as invalidating them as people, due in part to the overemphasis on their emotions. Therefore, adults must consider discussions with Gen Z that are more relational and less judgmental.

Certainly, Gen Z has to mature and accept the real world for what it is—and adults know it can be harsh. Although in previous generations, some parental coddling and stepping in to save a child from emotional distress existed, the extent to which it occurs today is exponentially greater. Parents must wean their children from this reliance and strive for greater balance between them and their children.

Parents also should find ways to engage their children toward the kind of maturity they expect. Disappointment is a good learning tool toward this end. As Gen Z matures, they will come to realize that through disappointment comes growth.

Acceptance of Gen Z by friends is very important to them. That is a given. But no friend can provide the same quality and depth of acceptance as a parent. A parent would be wise to capitalize on this. Gen Z is relational and values these relationships. Evidence of this fact is confirmed by a survey conducted by *Entrepreneur*. Forty-two percent of Gen Z surveyed stated that they respected their parents and that they followed their parents' advice on issues and tasks that life presents to them.[3]

Second, Gen Z places what they value on a pedestal, not unlike other generations. They clearly value what they believe in, but they are insecure about their beliefs. Indeed, they are very concerned about how well their beliefs are received.[4] The good news is that parents and other significant adults who demonstrate genuine interest in Gen Z's values have an advantage with them.

Take time to develop depth with Gen Z. Communicate the message that each of them possesses innate value—a message Gen Z needs to hear. Their emotions require regular validation. Reiterations of this kind of message are akin to mini-trophies for the easily bruised psyches and emotions of Gen Z children.

On the flip side, the educational climate today can be risky for professionals. Teachers who do not acknowledge the validity of some of the beliefs of Gen Z pay the price—they are labeled as intolerant or mean and hateful, or even lose their jobs. Social media is sometimes used vindictively, for emotional justification, often anonymously. Such was the case in Massachusetts, where the head of the oldest public school in the United States had to resign.

An offended group had reported "the incident to the headmaster and launched a social media campaign to tell the world they were unhappy with the response."[5] What was a local issue at a school went global.[6] The lesson to be learned is that people are going to accept Gen Z's values and concerns or pay a price with their career. Gen Z is unafraid to take a small message public, and technology makes it much easier both to help situations and to make them worse.[7]

Third, previous generations have much more experience than Gen Z in making life's decisions and economic choices for a future career.[8] Parents who take the time to share their wisdom through love and patience will meet with great respect from Gen Z. Empathy is a clear hallmark of this new generation.

Fourth, in the marketplace young Gen Z employees value the experience of veteran workers. Generally, they understand that they have much to glean from established employees. The opportunity to share these experiences with a generation of workers willing to work hard to achieve and advance is unique. Relating experience to Gen Z, then turning the workers of this generation loose, likely will result in many of them fulfilling their goals faster than previous generations. But first they have to put down their cell phones and learn some patience.

One reason for Gen Z's potential success in the workplace is their technological understanding and proficiency. They are learning how to leverage their drive and what they can bring to the economy through technology.[9] This will take some figuring, and the bumps in the road will be significant. Nevertheless, Gen Z is the "first truly mobile-first generation, so they place a big emphasis on personalization and relevance."[10]

Fifth, the time it takes to develop deep relationships is of paramount importance. Gen Z enjoys face-to-face interpersonal relationships, even as they are reluctant to put down their technology. So, in order for these interpersonal relationships to occur, Gen Z has to be given a choice. Either they limit their technology usage, or what they desire will not occur. Good intentions do not deepen relationships.

Gen Z must be convinced that the only way to arrive at the types of relationships they desire is to spend time together without distractions. They must develop patience. It can be done, and parents should demonstrate the importance of their children over their own technology. After all, Gen Z children have Gen Z parents. Therefore it is essential for parents and children to engage in discussions about balancing Gen Z's desires, its practices, and the real world. Parents understand better than anyone that relationships take time; lack of investment of this time will lead to certain social and relational issues later. No attempts at multitasking can accomplish what humans need in and from each other.

What Parenting Does Not Mean

Gen Z has a deep-seated belief of entitlement. As mentioned earlier in this book, many Gen Z parents do not allow their children to experience failure without (1) making excuses for them, or (2) stepping in to make things right for their children.

This mind-set of entitlement begins by parental over involvement as well as making certain that no one ever feels left out of activities, competitions, and events that award participants with equitable honors. Most of these things are practiced with the best of intentions. However, parenting does not mean rescuing children from all of their perceived needs and life's emotional dilemmas.

Showering children with material goods without their requiring effort to attain them sets them up for unrealistic expectations. This approach is less about partnering and more about feeding their entitlement mentality. Providing toys and technology at a child's every request in order to occupy their time or allow them emotional connections with friends may just escalate the problem over time.

With children, what is not earned usually is not deeply appreciated. Parents should determine early the consequences of incorporating digital devices into their children's lives—in brain development, sleep pattern interruptions, and overall behavior and mood swings.

The Digital Invasion

The introduction of communications technology today in many elementary schools affects children's behaviors in myriad ways. These changes become more vivid and are more deeply connected emotionally as children age. James Daly of *Focus on the Family* writes, "The 'digital invasion' is here. Along with it, we have teens with lower-than-average emotional intelligence and signs of technology-induced dementia, a rise in compulsive disorders and kids who don't know how to use their imaginations when they play."[11]

This is not what parenting and partnering with children are all about. In fact, pondering this, it appears the partnering is occurring with technology. When this happens, people tend to feel secondary to devices. However, as was stated earlier in this chapter, Gen Z desires face-to-face relationships. So, consider this question: What is being accomplished today by giving our children technology? Replacing a person with Facetime, Snapchats, or any other digital application certainly is not the type of partnering that is most beneficial to Gen Z children.

Along this line, Erica Diamond of *Women on the Fence* offers sage advice for Gen Z parents:

> With the large number of women in the workforce today, and parents more exhausted than ever before, moms and dads sometimes find themselves overcompensating for issues they feel guilty about . . . such as divorce, or working many hours. We've all been guilty of plopping our kids in front of baby Einstein just to get a moment's reprieve. But we as their parents are the role models. Children don't only learn by listening, they learn by watching. It is up to us to model proper behavior and practice restraint when it comes to demands placed upon us by Gen Zers. . . . They have to hear "no," sometimes, even when it is easier to say "yes." They have to get a little knocked down. We as their parents have to resist the urge to rescue them, and hover like helicopter parents. They have to experience failure. It is through failure that they grow—I can tell you from experience, failure is the biggest gift.[12]

Getting Better by Getting Worse?

Gen Z is prone to feeling depressed if their technology is taken away.[13] In fact, anecdotes abound of teenagers lashing out, even becoming violent, if a teacher or parent takes their smart phones for an extended period of time.[14] Furthermore, efforts to make everything fair for children, so that they don't experience failure or comparative weakness, sets them up for unrealistic expectations later. Sooner or later, things will have to change. In order to get better, attitudes and actions might first have to get worse. Given that Gen Z parents are compelled to fix things for their children, the irony of that looms large.

Schools Bail Out Gen Z Students

Take, for example, high schools that have done away with previous graduation requirements because parents and the community-at-large complained that too many
students were not graduating. The complaints were about levels of difficulty, about
exit exams that students did not pass. Today, students are graduating high school at
record rates, but not by improving their reading, math, or writing scores. The most
recent PISA scores indicate "U.S. Teenagers' Math Scores See [the] Greatest Drop
since 2009,"[15] the worst decline in nearly a decade. Specifically, the 2015 Program
for International Student Assessment, or PISA, "shows the U.S. with an 11-point
drop in the average score for math—the biggest decrease in the subject for American students since 2009, the last year that the score improved."[16] Math scores have
dropped, yet students are graduating in record numbers. Are you listening, parents?

Schools graduate students, in some cases, because adults want everyone to
have a diploma.[17] So counselors and administrators find alternative ways to hand
them one in order to show higher graduation rates. In some cases, teachers give
Gen Z breaks on class work, bending their own rules to pass them along. That is
detrimental to the students, their future, and the communities expecting that high
school graduates have a decent set of skills to enter the next phase of their lives.[18]

Partnering with Gen Z does not mean being their friend and giving them gifts.
Working and earning the things previous generations gained still rings true as the
main method of attaining goods in America. The time has come for parents to
consider the differences between helping Gen Z to be successful or bailing them
out when things are difficult.[19] Parents, schools, and even houses of worship must
join in the effort if we are to save Gen Z for the awesome future of their choosing.

PARTNERING WITH TEACHERS FOR ACCOUNTABILITY

Ask teachers what one thing might irk them about their students, then stand
back. Take the question of parental responses when teachers try to hold students
accountable. In today's system of public education, many parents are quick to
believe their children over their teachers, apparently trying to shield their children
from taking responsibility for what they say and do. Instead of parents and teachers working together as advocates, parents marginalize teachers far too often as
adversaries. The Gen Z children, then, are caught in the middle.

That's Unfair

Teachers who hold children accountable risk being singled out as unfair. Modern
parents tend to suffer from thinking more of their children than the reality presents. This may be what former Secretary of Education Arne Duncan had in mind
when referencing Common Core to a group of white suburban parents: "all of a
sudden—their child isn't as brilliant as they thought they were, and their school
isn't quite as good as they thought they were."[20]

Dr. Louis Profeta addresses this pressure placed on Gen Z by their parents, as well as their disappointment when injuries occur at young ages, in the parents' push for their children to be star athletes: "Your kids and my kids are not playing in the pros. . . . When I inform you as a parent that your child has just ruptured their ACL ligament or Achilles tendon, if the next question out of your mouth is, 'How long until he or she will be able to play,' you have a serious problem."[21] Similar questions are asked about academics, and reveal similar thinking. For example, the focus is simple to decipher when parents inquire, "What can my child do to make up all their work and raise their grades to be eligible?"

Teachers and parents may be hung up on the difference between "children" and "students." Until there is a meeting of the minds over what is expected and how best to work together, the parents of Gen Z and teachers may remain at odds. Teachers and parents can help each other, an approach explored later in this chapter.

Empowerment through Enablement

Enablement is commonly defined as providing a person with a certain level of empowerment, deemed adequate in authority, toward the accomplishment of one's desires, wishes, or goals. Educators refer negatively to students they believe to be enabled. Their understanding of the term implies an escape from accountability due to parental intervention. In reality, students are allowed to perpetuate a behavior that results in a student's personal advantage over a teacher or policy. That occurs daily in schools and, in context, is most often observed as a family member demonstrates personal empowerment against authority.

For example, take a parent who excuses a student's lack of responsibility in work or behavior, thereby creating in the student a vicarious sense of empowerment. The student then senses he or she has escaped consequences and often feels exempt from responsibility. Sometimes parents, with good intentions in the short run, set in motion expectations in their children that set them up for greater expectations and/or consequences in the long run. That is not in the best interest of the life and character of the Gen Z child.

Parents who cover for their children time and time again are not doing them any favors for their character development. Unfortunately, many of these actions are one-way streets of expectations on the part of the child, reinforcing the parental hierarchy in the child's life. Children raised on the premise that parents will always come to their rescue are realizing a poor precedent for their future involvement in college and career, which does not bode well for their independence down the road.

Empowerment through Technology

Children have learned how to use technology to complain to parents when life does not suit their desires. That use of technology to complain the moment a student feels insecure in a class, or when she has earned a grade lower than expected—even in the middle of a circumstance in which she is made to feel uncomfortable—is rampantly problematic. Smartphones often get in the way of classroom continuity and classroom management. Smartphones are students' "safe zones," which is one reason they react so angrily when their phones are confiscated for any period of time.

Once students graduate high school and move on into postsecondary education, the safe zones turn into "safe spaces." Unfortunately, setting in motion all of these safety nets does very little to help those protected from the more harsh realities that exist in life: the world, in fact, is unsafe.

Tricia Ferrara, author of *Parenting 2.0*, offers great advice for parents struggling with the demands of raising Gen Z. She declares, "Just folding and giving your children just what they want is not helpful for them over the long run . . . I know, for parents, sometimes it's easier for them . . . but easy for you is not healthy for them. So, teaching them or compelling them how to organize their energy toward a goal is critical. It's a critical skill for now, but it's a very critical skill for the future."[22]

GOVERNMENT IS IN THE WAY

Federal and state bureaucrats have gotten involved in child rearing. By making laws that usurp parental control and diminish parental roles and values, government officials are moving into the realm of child and family development. This usurpation takes many forms and plays out in different ways.

First, many parents are shamed if they raise their children with beliefs that are contrary to those supported by either the far right or far left. Second, some parents are called out, fined, and even arrested for standing firm on their beliefs and practices, which are declared intolerant and sometimes made illegal by bureaucrats. Those in government think they know best, so they pass legislation and policy that may be agenda driven. This political gnosis has become standard rhetoric on some school and college campuses, and is making headlines. For example, it is very easy to accuse someone of being a bully when one person makes another uncomfortable. Supporting one candidate over another during the 2016 presidential campaign was enough for some to claim they were made to feel unsafe, threatened by someone simply displaying a sign.[23]

Third, federal and state governments have a certain "nanny-state" mentality that brings additional usurpation of parental responsibilities. A "nanny-state" brings a clear message that "politicians and bureaucrats know more about how to live your life, manage your health, and raise your kids than you do."[24] For example, if a child needs food at school, the school provides it. If a child need medical care, the county or state provides it.

When transportation is needed, the government provides buses and vans. Class field trips often are paid for from a fund collected throughout the year. Special-needs students are tended to by aides or mainstreamed into classrooms.

Bilingualism is again becoming popular in some states in order to teach students in two languages. These examples are not meant as demeaning, only as examples of the government acting in loco parentis, doing what it thinks best for families and Gen Z children.[25]

Government bureaucracy has impacted public education overwhelmingly. Strings attached to funding have seen to it that public education in America has become a zero-sum game; decades of investment yielded a wasteland of broken educational paradigms. What is left is a mere shell encapsulating larger social and moral engineering designs on the next generation of students.

Bureaucrats have legislated and funded programs intended to modify the nature of humans. Students can no longer openly disagree on public school campuses with the current direction of social issues without the possibility of suspension. Psychologists call parents into question over their parenting. Where cultures disagree, parents and students are labeled haters and bigots. Is this what is in store for "post-truth" America, defining life by "relating to or denoting circumstances in which objective facts are less influential in shaping public opinion than appeals to emotion and personal belief?"[26] This appears to be the direction American schools are headed by emphasizing emotions over facts.

Social Engineering?

Gen Z is being engineered to accept and experiment with practices that a few short years ago were deemed highly controversial and outside the norm for many schools, faith communities, and businesses. Even as state bureaucrats, assisted mostly by partisan legislators, create these new environments, the inner city schools and communities are falling farther behind economically and educationally.

Add to these concerns the policing of families' uses of certain disciplinary methods not approved by the government, bringing fines and even arrests. Government has altered traditional marriage, legislated protection for newly defined genders, and in some cases requires professional development for schools to ensure that politically charged philosophies are established and protected.

An example of some psychologists' advocating for social engineering is found in the general belief today that no true differences are worth considering between boys and girls, and that gender is a mere construct. Furthermore, social engineering is occurring by assuring all teachers they possess unconscious bias toward minority children, and that some Americans experience privilege over others because of race. Gen Z is being exposed to social engineering unlike anything parents have experienced, and children are made to feel guilty for being who they are and what their parents taught them. Whatever happened to education? Hopefully, under the Every Student Succeeds Act (ESSA), some semblance of balance will return to American public education, beginning in our local communities.

Government has become the problem, not the solution. The words of Roger Pilon of the CATO Institute illustrate this point: "At its writing, the Constitution was a document of enumerated powers, with a vast sea of private liberty reserved. Today, it is a vast sea of powers lapping at islands of liberty."[27] Parents are losing freedom to raise their children as they see fit, and social engineering is happening right before their very eyes. Public education is complicit in this engineering.

CREATING RELIANCE CREATES ALLIANCE

The question parents must ask is whether the focal point of public education is now the creation of family reliance on government, so as to make certain that such government reliance cannot be abridged without great outcry. It will be a sad day when schools must be the arbiters of social conditioning and act as the primary family units for some children. Trauma and victimization are quite real for some children. Addictions, abuses, divorces, and a culture tolerant of far too many cultural changes have resulted in a seismic shift in the family. Schools today have stepped into this messy reality, and government now has an ally in the families requiring assistance. Can they be faulted for caring?

Anyone with an eye on education, who is in touch with the pulse of American culture, understands social aspects provide evidence that our culture could never have tolerated more rigorous education. Schools have become far too busy raising children, meeting their psychological and medical needs, and feeding them meals. Without stable families, rigor at school is just a political catch phrase.

Common sense says that classroom behaviors and deep-seated cultural concerns are not overcome by more difficult and challenging methods of learning.[28] If rigor is needed anywhere, it is basically to keep students in class. Is this the only hope of reaching them and saving their lives? What has America come to, that schools are doing the work of churches, but churches are only allowed to help in small social ways? Our nation certainly is not relying on schools solely for education.

Educators did not sign up for classroom triage. Likewise, they did not sign up to be a psychologists, or policemen, or even parents. Schools that take on these roles, yet do not allow the additional elements that round out the job titles, are realizing only minimal benefits. For example, if a young man needs a father figure, or mentor, the teacher is not allowed to impart his "fatherly values" to the child for fear he will offend someone. As a result, that inability to impart values disables the very approaches expected to make a difference.

It is not sensible to be told to make a difference in the lives of children in need, but not in genuine ways that can make a difference. It is equally unfair to a child to promote such mentorship, yet not allow the mentors the support to become a genuine ally for the child.

It's a Struggle for Many

Mental illness, victims of abuse, sexual identity, broken families, drug and alcohol addiction, and a raft of other concerns get in the way of being able to teach.

Teachers generally are hopeful creatures, usually to a fault. This hope is increasingly being tested as teachers' best efforts result in plummeting test scores, falling literacy rates, and newly funded government programs that cause social and economic dependency.

Examples of the Divide

In terms of classroom management, teachers are now given directives not to send kids to their school offices for offenses once deemed worthy of suspension or expulsion. Poorly behaving students are challenges to teachers. Parents understand that their children struggle, even if most do not admit it. Profanity, anger, and violent tendencies enter the classroom daily. If anyone thinks these problems are found only in high schools, they are sorely mistaken. Second graders demonstrate those same behaviors.

Gen Z parents have their hands full. Despite laws to the contrary—and school policies that require teachers to manage student behaviors in class—suspensions and expulsions are up. They are up for grades K–2 in some districts.[29] They are up in elementary, middle, junior high, and high school. Teachers are finding it harder to teach. Gen Z parents are discovering that the government parent with which they are allied is not parenting. The Gen Z parent is frustrated on two levels. Their children are lacking in education and in child rearing.

We have problems, America, and making education a more challenging place will do little to erase the issues that present themselves each day in the lives of those we call students. There is this slow dance between public education and American parents. As long as the music is playing, everyone thinks all is well. However, American education is missing the mark. Valerie Strauss writes what could very well be a defining statement about Gen Z and ways to recalibrate optimism and a new perspective in context for parents and teachers.

> When you see children who do not learn well in school, they will often display characteristics that would be valued and admired if they lived in any number of traditional societies around the world. They are physically energetic; they are independent; they are sociable; they are funny. They like to do things with their hands. They crave real play, play that is exuberant, that tests their strength and skill and daring an endurance; they crave real work, work that is important, that is concrete, that makes a valued contribution. They dislike abstraction; they dislike being sedentary; they dislike authoritarian control. They like to focus on the things that interest them, that spark curiosity, that drive them to tinker and explore.[30]

MENTORING PARENTS TO BENEFIT GEN Z STUDENTS

Aside from schools, civic organizations and faith communities often seem best positioned to assist families in their local communities. Serving families can be accomplished by means of cross-partnerships. Children go to school each day and are exposed to technology of some sort. Today's families with younger Gen Z children comprise a larger proportion of people on government subsistence than families in recent decades. However, programs have provided access to or possession of cell phones and computers to just about every student in America. This is a good thing.

Parents from all families have come to rely on their children's schools for assistance beyond education. Community school models are popping up all over, as these models are tied to local control funding formulas. These community schools are beginning to mark the educational landscape in states such as California and are often funded by donors willing to donate community services at no charge to students and families.

Under the ESSA, there are "provisions to support community schools, and will provide $6 million in grants"[31] to establish and begin some of the social and need-based programs. Block grants may be allocated to newly developed local agencies to assist families in need.

Posnick-Goodwin writes, "Schools don't need to pay high costs for these social services if they partner with public agencies, nonprofits or local colleges."[32] Everything from testing for sexually transmitted diseases, mental health counseling, abortion services, and insurance enrollment under the Affordable Care Act to meals, dental care, and a host of other services is available through community schools that partner with the community to care for the whole child.[33] Essentially, schools in this model are local families' all-in-one family surrogate and support network. Is this the new model for the American family? All of this may change under the Trump administration.

Parents should take advantage of the expertise and knowledge of teachers beyond their content knowledge. They should also become part of the civic and faith communities that join forces with schools on wider bases. In the nation's past, the majority of social change began in the churches. Today, the efforts are left to the halls of Congress, state bureaucrats, and elected officials seeking reelection time and time again. These entities are far too large to succeed. True change is internal and life altering, not left to a program supported by one political party or another.

GEN Z IS DIFFERENT FROM OTHER GENERATIONS

Families could benefit by attending places of worship to find spiritual mentorship and assistance. Some of what ails our nation today is a malaise over things spiritual. The rediscovery of a larger moral purpose for families often can be realized by reflecting on one's spiritual life. Schools are not supposed to focus on this, yet these same schools are under a mandate to educate the whole child. We must see to it that their families are cared for in places that care for their needs. Churches across America are ready and willing.

Gen Z students are different than students in previous generations, for several reasons.

- Cultural institutions have aggressively gone after children, exposing them to and pushing acceptance of behaviors, practices, and lifestyles that were unacceptable and even illegal a few years ago.
- Students are taught today from a foundation of psychology and philosophy that emotions are the most reliable arbiters of truth and understanding.
- With smart technology, students can access data, find answers, and explore their interests within seconds.
- Social media and instantaneous access to people anywhere in the world have resulted in a vast change in daily business.
- Gen Z's brain wiring is very different in terms of excitement, distractibility, boredom, and speed of processing.
- Children of Gen Z are not dedicated to depth of knowledge generally and are satisfied with less face-to-face communication.
- Speed of access to things digital is exhilarating to Gen Z.
- Gen Z loves to socialize, and would prefer to socialize through the avenue of brief staged videos and posed photos. Their philosophy easily could be reduced to the slogan "Online, everyone is a rock star."

Partnering for the success of Gen Z today requires knowledge of some of the basic differences between generations, as well as what specifically sets Gen Z apart. As detailed in chapters 2 and 3, some characteristics blend with the millennial generation; others are unique and distinct, comprising the very nature of Gen Z.[34]

WORKING WITH GEN Z CHILDREN

Parenting that worked a decade or two ago did not have to contend with device addiction or the colossal, always-on digital connectivity so prevalent among children today.

Consider the 1990s: Few students had cell phones on school campuses, and personal computers were gaining in popularity. A parent would phone or maybe e-mail a teacher to see how a student was performing. Many pieces of school literature were mailed home via the post office. Today, a teacher would be hard-pressed to find a student without a cell phone. Why should this be an added concern for schools?

Emphasis on the larger educational-technology components for the classroom is diminishing, while the more social components are culturally on the increase. This might be a wonderful thing for education, if used appropriately. Smartphones are mini-computers and contain a world of power for teachers as educational tools. However, their use in class comes with certain associated risks.[35]

Parenting always will mean being present in the lives of children. Parents should reflect on how they were parented, because "how you were parented is going to affect how you parent your children."[36] Likewise, parenting comes from feeling supported by others investing time in children. Parenting, as a rule, is very difficult, and it does not simply emerge "just by reading a book or going to the web."[37]

Recent Immigrants

Particularly difficult times exist for recent immigrants to America. Often children gain a much better grasp of the English language as they become immersed in American culture at school. Parenting in a different nation within a different culture can be extremely frustrating at times.[38] As Americans, the nation owes it to the most recent emigres to assimilate them into American culture, a process that usually is expedited through children.

By the time Gen Z children turn eighteen, they will have spent thousands of hours playing video games and becoming one with their screens. This includes the children of recent immigrants who have come to the United States as young children. Parenting from any culture that understands there are times to disengage from the digital realm, and consciously choose the interpersonal realm, is conscientious parenting. This will benefit children greatly.

The ubiquity of technology and the temptations that come with devices can be wedges in family time. A family that powers down their devices at scheduled times empowers itself. Those who leave them off during sleep hours will find greater balance and certainly will be better rested to face the challenges that lie ahead.

A Few Basic Guidelines

A few basic guidelines can help families wrestle with the challenges associated with technology. First, parents must understand what they have created in providing smartphones for their children and not be surprised to find out that their children are addicted to the devices they provided for them. As mentioned throughout this book, steps can be taken to reduce Gen Z children's reliance on the devices. In many cases, this reliance might best be minimized by parents demonstrating self-limitation.

Technology is a tool, and parents must revisit their personal and family philosophies regarding these tools. Remember, today's Gen Z views their cell phones as their lives. They are, in reality, *virtual*, and the smartphones are their emotional DNA.[39] For example, when a child takes ill, most examine the symptoms and draw certain conclusions. A visit to the family physician or the health clinic often reveals what is wrong with the child. Sometimes, the physician prescribes a medication to assist the child in his or her healing.

A similar situation exists today with children and their devices. Parents should watch their children closely. What they will see are children who often are tuned out, their head's tilted down in that all-too-familiar tech-neck slouch. Watch school-age children as they wend their way to school. See the potential danger as they saunter across streets without looking, or ride skateboards or bicycles with their ears budded. These are norms today. Inattentiveness toward the real world does much more damage than destroying digital creatures in video games. It can be deadly.

Something is wrong when children are in a trance-like state, unaware of their surroundings. How many parents are lulled into thinking that because a child is quiet that she is peacefully compliant, or that he is engaged in active learning? Quietude is not always a safe state.

Parental Diligence

Parents need to have authority over their children's devices. Parents need passwords to phones, computers, iPads, and anything else that commands the ultimate privacy of a child. Children can't have secret places to hide from parents the very things that may be causing them harm, especially if parents are paying for the devices and connectivity.

Parents should check on how often smartphone Internet searches occur; what websites are visited; which Snapchat videos were taken, sent, and received; and the times of day and night children are on their devices. Parents can see their children's phone activity and even read their text message archives online. Check with the service provider to access links on their websites.

Here is a warning: Once parents get serious and attentive to their children's technology use, Gen Z children will become more protective. Get ready for tantrums, extreme agitation, and proclamations of privacy violations. Parents will be called names and accused of distrust.

Would any parent ever provide something for their child just to elicit these responses? These are unintended consequences of providing technology for children without strict guidelines and their reinforcements. Over time, the outbursts may die down. Gen Z students' grades may increase, and necks may straighten. To move in this direction, consider the family technology self-reflection checklist.

GEN Z FAMILY AND TECHNOLOGY SELF-REFLECTION CHECKLIST

- Does my child need a smartphone? If not, why does it seem like there is a need for one?
- If your child asks for a smart device, what are the reasons he gives?
- On a scale of 1–10, with 10 as the highest, how important is it that your child obtains a cell phone?

- How many hours a day does my child engage in online activity, including at school and at home?
- Do you know which sites your child visits each day?
- Have you seen any photos taken by your child that are stored on the cell phone, in the Cloud, or posted on social media sites?
- Are you aware of any adults your child communicates with on his or her devices?
- How many devices do your children have, and why?
- In what ways does technology assist you in parenting better?
- Do you see personality changes in your child from extended use online, playing video games, or emotional situations caused by communicating with friends?
- Do you have any suspicions or indications that your child is addicted to his device or is moving in that direction?
- How do you plan to make certain your child's use of technology is balanced with other areas of his or her life?
- Are you partnering with your child's school, local faith community, or civic organization to address existing needs?
- Are you part of an online community that offers assistance with questions you might have in raising your family?
- To what extent does technology assist special-needs children in your family?
- What questions do you ask yourself before allowing your child to have a device for 24/7 connectivity?
- Which community groups, churches, synagogues, and schools provide evening parenting classes or after-school parental support for families today?

CONCLUSION

Gen Z parenting is a challenge today, and parents may be helped significantly by reaching out to institutions other than their schools. So many wonderful traits characterize Gen Z children, but their use of technology is keeping some of these traits from full development.

Teachers and parents can partner to help Gen Z succeed beyond their wildest imaginations. However, both must learn how to use modern technology to their advantage. This means that teachers should be informed about the technology that Gen Z incorporates into their lives daily, and parents must realize their children are using devices for social and entertainment reasons that far surpass texting.

The development of community between generations can be accomplished when teachers, parents, and students collaborate on projects that use Gen Z's interests. Publishing on the Internet is a wonderful way for students and teachers to interact. Google Classroom is a good tool to move in this direction. Working with others is a skill necessary for twenty-first-century job applicants.

Gen Z values volunteering experience and work experience, especially those with a social purpose that allow multitasking through technology. Gen Z job applicants prefer to meet personally with people for interviews, rather than through e-mail or other technology. Older Gen Z students, especially those now graduating from college or who have entered the workforce, are coming to terms with modifications of device knowledge. Gen Z seem to prefer working for mid-size corporations but are concerned with workplace conflicts between them, baby boomers, and Gen Xers.[40]

Gen Z value higher education but would prefer education be approached more unconventionally, whereas educators favor the models Gens X and Y used. Offline learning and entertainment appeal to Gen Z. They seek to be educated in order to fulfill a social responsibility, and a good number of Gen Zers think seriously about working for themselves.

Finally, Gen Z value the traditional notion of the American dream—purchasing a home, a car, and having enough discretionary cash to spend on themselves, trying their best to steer clear of exorbitant debt as well as put money away for the future. Different from previous generations Gen Z pay a bit more attention to economics, especially as it pertains to debt. In terms of the older students in the Gen Z population, compared with all previous generations, their average weekly cash allowance ranks much higher, as does their discretionary cash.[41]

We can only wait to see what transpires in the next decade for Gen Z and the impacts they will have on culture, family, and economics.

NOTES

1. Emily Hopkins, "Raising Generation Z: What the Experts Say," *Cambridge Center for Families*, August 10, 2016. http://scoutcambridge.com/raising-generation-z-what-the -experts-say/. Retrieved August 28, 2016.

2. 1 Timothy 4:12.

3. Nina Zipkin, "Here's What the Future of Work Looks Like to Millennials and Generation Z," *Entrepreneur*, June 8, 2015. https://www.entrepreneur.com/article/247115. Retrieved November 3, 2016.

4. Zipkin, "Here's What the Future of Work Looks Like to Millennials and Generation Z."

5. Lynne Mooney Tata, "Head of Oldest U.S. Public School Resigns Amid Race Scandal," *CBS News*, June 22, 2016. http://www.cbsnews.com/news/boston-latin-high-school -headmaster-resigns-civil-rights/. Retrieved June 22, 2016.

6. Tata, "Head of Oldest U.S. Public School Resigns Amid Race Scandal."

7. Tata, "Head of Oldest U.S. Public School Resigns Amid Race Scandal."

8. Zipkin, "Here's What the Future of Work Looks Like to Millennials and Generation Z."

9. Giselle Abramovich, "Fifteen Mind-Blowing Stats about Generation Z," *CMO Adobe*, June 12, 2015. http://www.cmo.com/features/articles/2015/6/11/15-mind-blowing -stats-about-generation-z.html#gs.8hsD_Vw. Retrieved November 3, 2016.

10. Abramovich, "Fifteen Mind-Blowing Stats about Generation Z."

11. James Daly, "Protecting Your Family from the Digital Invasion," *Focus on the Family Daily Focus*, December 31, 2013. http://jimdaly.focusonthefamily.com/protecting-your-family-from-the-digital-invasion/. Retrieved November 4, 2016.

12. Erica Diamond, "Are You Raising a Generation Z'er?" *Women on the Fence*, October 3, 2013. http://womenonthefence.com/page/35/?__hstc=179794427.f266a3d f2edb7f7e72e9b5a9f4c4c806.1472601600061.1472601600063.1472601600064.2&__hss c=179794427.1.1472601600064&__hsfp=1773666937. Retrieved August 28, 2016.

13. Abramovich, "Fifteen Mind-Blowing Stats about Generation Z."

14. John Hadden, "Student Punches Teacher Repeatedly after Cellphone Taken Away," *Global News*, September 8, 2015. http://globalnews.ca/news/2210431/student-punches-teacher-repeatedly-after-cell-phone-taken-away/. Retrieved November 3, 2016.

15. Tawnell D. Hobbs, "U.S. Teenagers Lose Ground in International Math Exam, Raising Competitiveness Concerns," *Wall Street Journal*, December 6, 2016. http://www.wsj.com/articles/u-s-teenagers-lose-ground-in-international-math-exam-raising-competitiveness-concerns-1481018401. Retrieved December 8, 2016.

16. Hobbs, "U.S. Teenagers Lose Ground in International Math Exam, Raising Competitiveness Concerns."

17. Valerie Strauss, "What the Modern World Has Forgotten about Children and Learning," *Washington Post*, August 19, 2016. https://www.washingtonpost.com/news/answer-sheet/wp/2016/08/19/what-the-modern-world-has-forgotten-about-children-and-learning/. Retrieved August 23, 2016.

18. Susan Edelman, "High School's New Policy Would Allow Failing Students to Pass," *New York Post*, July 17, 2016. http://nypost.com/2016/07/17/high-schools-new-policy-would-allow-failing-students-to-pass/. Retrieved July 17, 2016. Cf. Sharon Noguchi, "California Exit Exam Abolished, Diplomas To Be Awarded," *San Jose Mercury*, October 8, 2015. http://www.mercurynews.com/california/ci_28936216/exit-exam-abolished-diplomas-be-awarded. Retrieved July 17, 2016. Cf. also Kyle Rothenberg, "Are High School Exit Exams Necessary? More States Are Saying No," *Fox News*, April 3, 2015. http://www.foxnews.com/us/2015/04/03/are-high-school-exit-exams-necessary-more-states-are-saying-no.html. Retrieved July 17, 2016.

19. Anne Boysen, "A Generation of Coddled Gladiators: A Paradox of Modern Parenting," *After the Millennials*, November 8, 2014. http://afterthemillennials.com/2014/11/08/a-generation-of-coddled-gladiators-a-paradox-of-modern-parenting/. Retrieved November 3, 2016.

20. Valerie Strauss, "Arne Duncan: 'White Suburban Moms' Upset That Common Core Shows Their Kids Aren't Brilliant," *Washington Post*, November 16, 2013. https://www.washingtonpost.com/news/answer-sheet/wp/2013/11/16/arne-duncan-white-surburban-moms-upset-that-common-core-shows-their-kids-arent-brilliant/?utm_term=.d4eac5a52040. Retrieved December 8, 2016.

21. Louis Profeta, "Your Kid and My Kid Are Not Playing in the Pros," *Slow Family Living*, October 29, 2014. http://slowfamilyliving.com/2014/10/your-kid-and-my-kid-are-not-playing-in-the-pros/. Retrieved November 3, 2016.

22. Kathy Wallace, "Raising Spoiled Kids: How to Set Limits," *CNN*, June 23, 2016. http://www.cnn.com/2016/06/21/health/parent-acts-spoiled-children-how-to-say-no/index.html. Retrieved June 23, 2016. Cf. Tricia Ferrara, *Parenting 2.0: Think in the future, Act in the Now* (Austin, TX: Greenleaf Book Group Press, 2014).

23. Michelle Moons, "Arizona Mexican Restaurant Owner Threatened over Donald Trump Sign," *Breitbart*, March 23, 2016. http://www.breitbart.com/big-government/2016/03/23/arizona-mexican-restaurant-owner-threatened-over-donald-trump-sign/. Retrieved November 3, 2016.

24. Editors' Commentary, "The Nanny State," *CATO Institute*, May 27, 2015. https://www.cato.org/research/nanny-state. Retrieved November 3, 2016.

25. Todd A. DeMitchell, "In Loco Parentis," *United States Education Law*, n.d. http://usedulaw.com/345-in-loco-parentis.html. Retrieved November 3, 2016.

26. "Word of the Year 2016: Post-truth," *Oxford Dictionary*. https://en.oxforddictionaries.com/word-of-the-year/word-of-the-year-2016. Retrieved December 9, 2016.

27. Roger Pilon, "A Vast Sea of Federal Power, Lapping at Islands of Freedom," *CATO Institute Insight*, December 12, 1994. https://www.cato.org/publications/commentary/vast-sea-federal-power-lapping-islands-freedom. Retrieved December 9, 2016.

28. Ernest J. Zarra III, *Common Sense Education: From Common Core to ESSA and Beyond* (Lanham, MD: Rowman & Littlefield, 2016), 20–21.

29. "Children Still Suspended in High Numbers Despite New Law," *Hartford Courant*, July 18, 2016. http://www.chron.com/news/education/article/Children-still-suspended-in-high-numbers-despite-8384191.php. Retrieved July 18, 2016.

30. Strauss, "What the Modern World Has Forgotten about Children and Learning."

31. Sherry Posnick-Goodwin, "Caring for the Whole Child," *California Educator* 21(3) (October 2016): 21.

32. Posnick-Goodwin, "Caring for the Whole Child," 20–21.

33. Posnick-Goodwin, "Caring for the Whole Child," 16–21.

34. Dan Schawbel, "Fifty-one of the Most Interesting Facts about Generation Z," *Dan Schawbel's Blog*, July 17, 2014. http://danschawbel.com/blog/39-of-the-most-interesting-facts-about-generation-z/. Retrieved August 28, 2016.

35. Ernest J. Zarra III, *Teacher-Student Relationships: Crossing into the Emotional, Physical, and Sexual Realms* (Lanham, MD: Rowman & Littlefield, 2013), 100–101.

36. Emily Hopkins, "Raising Generation Z: What the Experts Say," *Cambridge Center for Families*, August 10, 2016. http://scoutcambridge.com/raising-generation-z-what-the-experts-say/. Retrieved August 28, 2016.

37. Hopkins, "Raising Generation Z."

38. Hopkins, "Raising Generation Z."

39. Zarra, *Teacher-Student Relationships*, 100–101.

40. Schawbel, "Fifty-one of the Most Interesting Facts about Generation Z."

41. Schawbel, "Fifty-one of the Most Interesting Facts about Generation Z."

Index

About the Author

Ernest J. Zarra III teaches college preparatory U.S. government and politics and economics to seniors at the state-decorated and top-ranked Centennial High School in Bakersfield, California. Zarra has five earned degrees and holds a PhD from the University of Southern California, in teaching and learning theory, with cognates in psychology and technology. He is a former Christian College First Team All-American soccer player, former teacher of the year for the prestigious Fruitvale School District, and was awarded the top graduate student in education from the California State University at Bakersfield.

Zarra has written six books, including *The Entitled Generation: Helping Teachers Teach and Reach the Minds and Hearts of Generation Z* (Rowman & Littlefield, 2017), *Common Sense Education: From Common Core to ESSA and Beyond* (Rowman & Littlefield, 2016), *The Wrong Direction for Today's School: The Impact of Common Core on American Education* (Rowman & Littlefield, 2015), and *Teacher-Student Relationships: Crossing into the Emotional, Physical, and Sexual Realms* (Rowman & Littlefield, 2013).

Dr. Zarra has written more than a dozen journal articles and professional development programs. He is a national conference presenter, former district professional development leader, adjunct university instructor, and a member of several national honor societies. Originally from New Jersey, he and his wife, Suzi, also a teacher, and their two adult children, have resided in California for most of their adult lives.